I Like
Being®
Married

———⋙———

I Like Being® Married

~∞~

Treasured Traditions,
Rituals, and Stories

Edited by

Michael Leach and

Therese J. Borchard

IMAGE BOOKS / DOUBLEDAY

New York   London   Toronto   Sydney   Auckland

AN IMAGE BOOK
PUBLISHED BY DOUBLEDAY
a division of Random House, Inc.

IMAGE, DOUBLEDAY, and the portrayal of a deer drinking from a stream are
registered trademarks of Random House, Inc.

I Like Being® is a registered trademark of Michael Leach and Therese J. Borchard.
Other books in the I Like Being® series include: *I Like Being® Catholic, I Like
Being® American, I Love Being a Mom.*
I Like Being® Married was published in hardcover by Doubleday in 2002.

Pages 219–24 consist of an extension of this copyright page.

Book design by Donna Sinisgalli

The Library of Congress has cataloged the hardcover edition as follows:
I like being® married : treasured traditions, rituals, and stories / edited by Michael
Leach and Therese J. Borchard.
p. cm.
1. Marriage—Miscellanea. 2. Love—Miscellanea. I. Leach, Michael, 1940– .
II. Borchard, Therese Johnson.
HQ734 .I2 2002
306.81—dc21   2001047155

ISBN-13: 978-0-385-50232-0

ISBN-10: 0-385-50232-X

146484122

FOR
VICKIE AND ERIC

It is only with the heart
that one can see rightly;
what is essential
is invisible to the eye.

Antoine de St. Exupéry

CONTENTS

Contents

Contents

Contents

Contents

Contents

I Like
Being®
Married

———⸎———

—— ⌘ ——

I LIKE BEING MARRIED

What do Paul Newman and Joanne Woodward, Jimmy and Rosalynn Carter, and Cokie and Steve Roberts have in common with 112 million Americans from Bangor, Maine, to Burbank, California? They like being married, and they don't mind saying so. Many of them share delicious slices of their memories, experiences, and insights in this wedding cake of a book.

I Like Being® Married celebrates the treasured traditions, rituals, and stories that run through the bloodstreams of married couples everywhere. Martin Luther wrote five centuries ago: "There is no more lovely, friendly, and charming relationship, communion, or company than a good marriage."

Cynics say that conventional marriage is as outdated and restrictive as the Gutenberg printing press of Luther's time. But despite the trash talk on TV scream-fests, polls show that the average American adult not only *is* married but *likes* being married. "Chains do not hold a marriage together," says Simone Signoret. "It's threads, hundreds of tiny threads, which sew people together through the years."

This book is a patchwork quilt sewn with the threads that bind couples who are famous and those who live next door, threads of commitment that bind them as one. A good marriage is a blanket of love that gives comfort, assurance, and impulse to say three of the most powerful sentences in the English language: "I love you," "Thank you," and "I do."

From wedding day to widowhood, *I Like Being® Married* reminds us of promises kept and love that endures. Each testimony, story, or insight affirms a value or truth that time cannot tarnish. Artists, poets, and troubadours have always celebrated marriage on canvas, paper, and film. This book spotlights memorable movies, novels, songs—and even TV sitcoms—

that inspire us to see marriage with fresh eyes and a warm heart. They remind us of the good that we already know but too often forget to cherish.

At heart, then, this book is about what the philosopher Pierre Teilhard de Chardin called "the chosen part of things." It endeavors to show, in word and picture, with pride and joy, the qualities of marriage that transcend appearances. It is not a "how to" guide, but a "what is" appreciation. As psychiatrist Thomas Hora said, "If you know what, you know how."

The couples you'll meet in *I Like Being® Married* have learned *what*. And they know *how*. Here then is a window into their hearts. We invite you to look in and learn why—after five, ten, twenty-five, or fifty years—they *still* say, "I like being married!"

—Michael Leach and Therese J. Borchard
January 2002

The Right Question

Many couples ask themselves, "Should we get married or shouldn't we get married?" This is the wrong question. The right question is, "What is marriage?" If we know what marriage is, if we have a clear understanding of what an existentially valid marriage is, then the right action will be easier to follow.

Marriage is neither political, socioeconomic, sexual, nor legal; it is primarily an existential situation. What do we mean by that? "Existential" means that the real issue in marriage is living under the most favorable and fulfilling conditions. The institution of marriage is ideally designed to improve the quality of life for both husband and wife, and their offspring, by creating a harmonious unit.

Marriage is not a place to fight for equal rights, it is not a battleground for ego gratification, or an arena for power-madness. Marriage is a situation where the beautiful, the good, the harmonious, and intelligent life can be cultivated and realized. It is a joint participation in the good of God.

—Thomas Hora, M.D.

First, God's love.
And next . . . the love of wedded souls,
Which still presents that mystery's counterpart.

—Elizabeth Barrett Browning

Nothing is more practical than finding God, that is, than falling in love in a quite absolute, final way. What you are in love with, what seizes your imagination, will affect everything. It will decide what will get you out of bed in the morning, what you do with your evenings, how you spend your weekends, what you read, who you know, what breaks your heart, and what

amazes you with joy and gratitude. Fall in love, stay in love, and it will decide everything.

—Pedro Arrupe

First we fall in love. That's the exciting part. Then we learn to love. That's
the hard part. Finally, we simply love being loving. And that, by far, is the
best part.

—Michael Leach

MARRIAGE *IS*

> *The most beautiful things in the world*
> *are not seen or touched,*
> *they are felt with the heart.*
> *Helen Keller*

Before you become interested in seeing the light, to you mountains are mountains and waters are waters; after you get an insight into reality, mountains to you are no longer mountains and waters are no longer waters; but after this when you really attain the place of peace, mountains are once more mountains and waters are waters.

—Old Zen saying

Same old slippers,
Same old rice,
Same old glimpse of
Paradise.

—William James Lampton

My husband is my best friend. When I wake up and look at him next to me, I smile. He is a good man and a gift of God to me.
—Carmen Rodriguez
Monticello, New York

⤫

Squinching

BY PHYLLIS A. TICKLE

One pleasantly cool morning a few weeks ago, I was lying in bed not quite awake and not quite asleep, but just drifting in that state which is halfway between the two. I was thinking of nothing more significant and meaningful than how good the blanket felt up around my shoulders and that the tip of my nose was just cold enough to feel good too. In the half-light seeping around the edges of the bedroom shades, I could tell from the faint smile on his face that Sam was floating in the same delicious suspension as I was. At the time, he was on his back, which meant that I was lying in my favorite position as well. On my left side with my knees drawn up half under his buttocks and my torso shoved solidly up against his, I had my left arm tucked under me and my neck cradled on top of his outstretched right arm. My right hand lay flat on top of his chest, secured by the tight, warm grip of his left one.

It was, as I have said, a perfectly lovely moment. I would even say a perfectly ordinary one, were it not that something in me rebels at the notion of the words *lovely* and *ordinary* being in the same sentence together without any explanation. Be that as it may, however, we were lying there in customary positions and totally familiar circumstances when it happened. I was watching Sam's face, trying to gauge just how awake he really was and how much longer we were going to be able to fend off reality by lying there like truant children. He still had his eyes closed—a good and hopeful sign, I thought—and his breathing was still reassuringly even and deep . . . or it was, until abruptly he did this thing. *He squinched.*

Yes, he squinched. The side of his nose from its beginning at the inside edge of his cheek to the peak of its bridge wrinkled up like corduroy. Not another facial muscle moved, not another piece of skin twitched, just that thin, tightly drawn bit from cheek base to bridge.

"That's not possible," I thought and realized that I was abruptly awake. Then just as I had almost persuaded myself that no one could even do what I thought he had done, Sam Tickle up and did it again . . . which pretty much says it all for me. That is, I had been lying beside that same man in that same position for almost fifty years and he had never once squinched before. I mean, just as I was beginning to think I had it all figured out at last, the man goes and takes up squinching. I was appalled and, for several days thereafter, I continued to be offended . . . no so much at Sam, you understand, as at a system that lets a person change his personal habits after fifty years and not even have to apologize for it. I got up grumpy and stayed that way for a good five minutes before the whole thing struck me as being as funny as it was annoying.

When I was a maturing teenager, my mother used to say, "Marriage *is*" when considering such moments and she'd stop the sentence right there. For all my pestering, she would never add either predicate nominative or predicate adjective to her statement. She would just shake her head and simply repeat "Marriage is" as if that were the whole sum of the thing. Since the squinching episode, I have begun to accept the authenticity of her statement and, almost, to appreciate its sufficiency.

My mother's other great pronouncement on the subject of marriage was that married people, men and women alike, could all be divided into two groups. There were those, she said, who were constantly conscious of their marriages at some varying level of awareness, and then there were those who were totally unaware of their married state, much less of its being a freestanding part of themselves. By this she meant something entirely different from what you and I would infer were she to say the words in our hearing today. That is, my mother was not speaking of flirtatious conduct or even of some casual naughtiness in the sheets, but of a kind of anesthetized indifference that sometimes characterized marriage in her times. With the exception of spinster aunts and older widows, almost everyone in my mother's

The beginning of a beautiful friendship...

day was married simply because, as she said, marriage *was,* just like eating was or sleeping was or earning a living and believing in something were. Marriage was as matter-of-fact a part of human existence as any other of these things, just as it was closely related to each of them by social expectation and outright necessity.

Times have changed, of course, and blessedly marriage is only one of several attractive and sustaining options open to us. Even fifty years ago when Sam and I took our vows, either or both of us could probably have bucked expectation and remained both single and still respected at one and the same time, had we chosen to do so. Certainly there's no doubt that any one of our children, boys and girls alike, could have opted out of marriage with never a word or a query from their peers, their employers, or their fellow citizens. In point of fact, three of them did take their own sweet time and almost thirty years of life before succumbing, though their grandmother, were she still around, would never, never be able to put them in her category of the unaware. Rather, delaying marriage has bred in them that kind of honed intentionality and focus that seem to me to be becoming hallmarks of marriage in these days of many options.

In point of fact, if I were to assume my mother's penchant for separating married people by types, I would have to confess that I can think right now of no more than two (maybe three) acquaintances who might possibly fit into her indifference column; and both of them are over fifty. Everybody else I can think of falls more or less into her category of the constantly aware. The difference between my effort at groupings and my mother's, then, is that I effectively have only *one* group . . . that, and the fact that my one big group has four parts. Of course, nobody I know ever stays in any one of my four boxes for more than a few days at a time, but it consoles me to have a sense of order about such things. All of which is to say that, unless my powers of observation fail me, the range of emotion among the married and aware today seems to swing on a rather frequent basis from "I hate being married to XYZ," to "I hate being married," to "I like being married," to those ebullient, euphoric moments of "I love being married to XYZ."

The interesting thing, now that I am old and can observe with more perspective if not objectivity, is that bouncing back and forth amongst these states of self-perception is not only normal, but even helpful. It is only the business of staying in any one of them for too long that seems to invite disease if not in one's self, then in one's mate, and certainly in one's marriage.

I rarely hate being married to Sam Tickle on Sunday, for instance. On Sunday, we get up late, we go to church, we go by his mill working plant to feed R.J., the guard dog with the perpetually happy disposition (Don't ask!), and we go out for a late, long lunch. What's not to like about that? As a schedule, it's predictable, low-key, and almost impeccably stressless. Because of that fact, most Sundays never come close to punching even one of my hot buttons. (Much as I may deplore those buttons, I still have to have them, and always at the ready, too.) But the point here is that on Sunday we're not at home, so Sam does not whine that somebody—meaning me—has misplaced his hammer or his hedge clippers or his checkbook, because on Sunday he's neither building nor gardening nor banking. On Sunday, I'm not reminded, as a consequence, that never in his life has the man ever lost anything or made a mistake that couldn't, and won't, be laid to my doing. Just ask him, but please don't do it on a Sunday.

The times I positively love being married to Sam Tickle are cut from a different run of cloth, however. They're the moments or hours or days when he's tending to a hurt animal or an errant and ailing plant; and I can feel the gentleness of his hands just by watching him. I can know, as well, that whatever he touches will be the better for his having laid his hands and his wisdom upon it. Retired now from the active practice of medicine, the man is and ever was a healer of all living things. There is about him, when he is practicing his art, a kind of magic that is as visible as a nimbus and that at times fills my eyes with tears with its beauty and economy.

I love being married to Sam Tickle and nobody else in the whole world ever when he is in conversation with other people and casually inserts flashes of insight or esoteric fact or introspective experience that neither I

nor anyone else present had either suspected in him or thought of for ourselves. The fact that he never knows he's executing this bit of legerdemain
only adds spice to the surprise of it. I love being married to Sam Tickle
when he's in his planning mode. What to do about Christmas decorations?
About the flower beds along the front walk this spring? About marketing
the end bits and pieces of prize lumber left over from the mill works?
Always there is the studied consideration of the possibilities followed by the
imperturbable concentration and focus in exploring and effecting the decisions followed always and without fail by a result which, while unusual and
sometimes even quirky, inevitably solves the problem with style and
panache. This latter result is blatantly remarkable, in fact. I know, because
other people besides me remark upon it rather frequently.

I love being married to Sam as Sam at other times too, of course. Most
of those times, however, belong not here in public conversation, but rather
in private ones between the two of us. Besides, like Sundays or the bene-
dictions of healing or the creative flashes of genius, such times are not the
warp and woof of marriage so much as they are the color and highlights in
its pattern. The steady weaving of a life together is caught and anchored
elsewhere. It is caught and anchored in the tension of the fast-moving shut-
tle as it flashes back and forth between "I hate being married in general" and
"I love being married in general."

For most of us there is nothing personal involved in the "I hate being
married" frame of mind that afflicts us from time to time. Rather, there is
a totally dispassionate, totally impersonal recognition on the part of many
a woman that it's a damned nuisance to have to do up whole baskets full of
laundry which she didn't dirty in the first place and most of which didn't
need to be dirtied quite so viciously and carelessly in the second place. It's
also a pain on most days for many a man to have to leave what he is doing
in order to eat, hungry or not, just because somebody else wants him to and
is more insistent than she has a right to be. It's a real unpleasantness for
everybody to be able to track a mate's progress through a house every single
day by the trail of open drawers, slightly ajar doors, and pieces of abandoned clothing he or she has left in his or her wake and intends always to
leave there. The result of these low-grade aberrations of conduct is that even
on Sundays, most of us can have fleeting, and sometimes less than fleeting,
moments of not liking to be married in general, if not in particular.

The times of our discontent are only adult versions, of course, of the contretemps between petulant two-year-old twins sharing the same sandbox or aggrieved adolescent siblings still sharing the same bathroom. We choose not to see our grown-up discomforts of inconvenience and limited autonomy in such terms, naturally, but that ego-protecting decision does not change the progress of what is happening to us. Like rocks in a lapidary's tumbler, husbands and wives are daily sanded and smoothed and pol-

Still the beginning of a beautiful friendship...

ished, each by the other; and abrasion by any name hurts. It also produces a fine patina, one that most of us can achieve in no way other than in the tumbler.

So, do I like being married? Yes, but unlike my mother's aphorism, I think marriage *does* as well as *is,* and I like being married for both those things.

Marriage makes me more than me (for we are two and formidably balanced in our skills) and less than me (for married I am only half a whole and no longer my own free agent).

It makes me strong to venture (for there is another waiting to catch and repair me) and weak to dare (for there is another whose good rises and falls with my own).

It makes me more sure (for there is another who has told me of the rightness of my thoughts) and less sure (for there is another who has demanded I see the error and selfishness of my ways).

It makes me Phyllis to his Sam, yet teases us both with the sure knowledge that his Sam has become my Phyllis and that, like the rocks in the tumbler, our surfaces now more reflect each other than their own singularities.

Having said that, however, I must add one last and purely personal note, namely that I have had to change my initial opinion of squinching. It is increasingly my opinion, in fact, that in an era where marriage both is and does, squinching and all its near-kin of random acts and brand-new gestures are really quite reassuring and valuable. Squinching, at least in my brief experience with it, seems to mean that even after half a century there's still some otherness in this marriage that wants courting and that wants to court. It would seem, in fact, that there's still some life in the old boy that I haven't yet discovered, much less worked on. As I say, I like being married both in general and in particular.

Phyllis Tickle is the author of *The Shaping of a Life: A Spiritual Landscape* and *The Divine Hours,* a three-volume contemporary Book of Hours. She and Sam, married in 1955, live, love, and squinch in Millington, Tennessee.

༺☒༻

The most precious gift that marriage gave me is this constant impact of something very close and intimate yet all the time unmistakably other, resistant—in a word, real.
—C. S. Lewis

Marriage is a promise made in the sight of God years ago and only yesterday. It is a promise kept day in, day out, for years and years, while two individuals become different people than when they first met, yet remain the same, until one of them takes their last breath. Before and after children, with and without children, even because of the children, marriage means they work together at everything from maximizing sexual joy to making the mortgage payments. They work hard at everything from doing the laundry to bringing home flowers in the middle of winter, whether the winter is seasonal or emotional. They made a promise, and marriage is a promise kept. Marriage is a couple who discovers a little bit more each day, to their surprise and delight and sometimes shock and chagrin, that in their togetherness and individuality they have an ongoing experience of intimacy with God. A God who is Love, and who inspires each of them together to become much more than they are.
—Mitch Finley
Spokane, Washington

Is there anything more sterling than fidelity, anything more uniquely and gloriously human than a promise made and kept? Within a universe of uncertainty, of stars searing into being and dying, mountain ranges rising and falling gradually away, continents shifting on their tectonic plates, of species of flora and fauna appearing and vanishing, within the uncertainties and dangers of life that have always been acknowledged—death and sickness, natural disasters, human cruelties, deprivations—how very necessary that human beings exert their ability to create something secure, a stable, dependable place of faith and love, a place where the strength to carry out constructive acts of generosity and compassion is engendered. Such a place can be created by an enduring marriage, by adherence to the life-promoting power of the promise of fidelity made and kept by husband and wife, and by both to the children of their union.

> —Pattiann Rogers
> Denver, Colorado

A lady of 47 who has been married 27 years and has six children knows what love really is and once described it to me like this: "Love is what you've been through with somebody."

> —James Thurber

Diana and I like being married best whenever we are aware of its helpful definition as "a joint participation in the good of God." Those moments when we focus on seeing and appreciating the spiritual values and qualities in each other, as well as in everyone and everything we encounter, transform our marriage into a blessing unmatched by any other perspective or relationship.

> —Bruce and Diana Kerievsky
> Great Neck, New York

I may not be smart, but I know what love *is*.

> —Forrest Gump

Now I know what love is.

> —Virgil

INTERLUDE

Some Advice from a Mother to Her Married Son

BY JUDITH VIORST

The answer to do you love me isn't, I married you, didn't I?
Or, Can't we discuss this after the ballgame is through?
It isn't, Well that all depends on what you mean by "love."
Or even, Come to bed and I'll prove that I do.
The answer isn't, How can I talk about love when the
*   bacon is burned and the house is an absolute mess*
*   and the children are screaming their heads off and*
*   I'm going to miss my bus?*
The answer is yes.
The answer is yes.
The answer is yes.

Chapter Two

——— ✥ ———

MARRIAGE *DOES*

It is when you give of yourself
that you truly give.
There are those who give
with joy,
and that joy is their reward.
Through the hands
of such as these
God speaks,
and from behind their eyes
God smiles upon the earth.

Kahlil Gibran

It is wonderful to get a bouquet of flowers from my husband, but it means even more when he gets me aspirin for my cramps. I can take my husband out for a fancy dinner, but it will not give him as much pleasure as my telling him that he looks sexy in his ratty pajamas. In a world that can feel cold and hostile, the value of marriage is that together you can create islands of "June" that comfort and sustain you the whole year through. The trick is in remembering to do it.

—Elizabeth Berg

Marriage inspires you to become a better person. If you let it, a wonderful alchemy takes place. Much like a sculptor crafts a statue from a block of stone, marriage chips away the idiosyncrasies and insecurities of each partner to reveal an unvarnished beauty and a simple goodness. A good marriage cuts away our self-centered genes, replaces them with a generous spirit, and transforms the ugliest of us into loving and lovable beings. Without my husband's love I fear the selfish tyrant I might have become. Marriage has done wonders for me, and I'm grateful.

—Therese J. Borchard

There are times when Kathy's goodness overwhelms me. Through her example of unselfish giving, she has made me a better husband, father, and person. I am a very lucky man.

—Tom Mannard
Arlington Heights, Illinois

You know that there is one person in this world you can always count on. They love you when you are down and they celebrate the good times with you. Your happiness is their happiness and your sorrow is their sorrow.

—Kathy Mannard
Arlington Heights, Illinois

You make me want to be a better man.

—Jack Nicholson in *As Good As It Gets*

❦

Ten Good Reasons to Be Married
BY PAUL WILKES

1. . . . Someone to grow old with
    . . . And stay young with.

A true marriage partner is a person who knows the sometimes rugged contours of my human landscape, a person who knows that inside me beats the heart of a teenager though the folds of my skin tell another story. Being married means that I can wake up each day—older, to be sure—but know that this is a person who will be there as the years both teach us and take their toll. What a wonderful comfort that is. Being married is being able to look back and smile at our successes and failures together and somehow know that both have forged this mysterious bond we have. And yet this is a person with whom I can make those funny sounds, use silly words that only the two of us know the precise meaning, behave in ways that recall when we were young, our love was fresh—but nowhere as deep as it has become over the years.

2. . . . Someone who tells me no
    . . . And says yes.

No to my foolishness, my impatience, my shortsightedness. *Yes* to my dreams, spoken and silent. Being married means having someone who, when I behave pitifully, has pity on me, then gently—and sometimes not so gently—brings me back to reality. Being married is having someone who can see over the next hill of my life and who assures me that, yes, dream, hope, reach. Why not? What kind of life would it be without those dreams? Being married means having someone who, like the Great Gatsby, sees me for the best I could ever imagine myself being.

3. . . . Someone to go to bed with at night
    . . . And to be apart from.

No, the first part of this equation is not about sex . . . usually.

It begins when the plane lands, the car is turned off, the door is opened, the soft light beneath the bedroom door spills out. It is about anticipation.

It is that tingle, that rush of "coming home." Then, it's the beauty and simplicity and comfort of laying down beside the same person each night. Having a toe or shoulder touch that same spot on another body, a place touched hundreds, thousands of times. Being able to rest, to put the day behind with someone who knows all that we are—and is not going anywhere but to sleep.

And the second part isn't about escape . . . usually. It is about understanding that sometimes I simply must be alone, and that my spouse should not take it personally; this is not rejection. There is a path I must walk alone, a room I must sit in—alone. I carry my spouse's love everywhere, but there are times when only in my aloneness can I think, be, and act.

4. . . . *Someone to raise children with*
   . . . And to be alone with.

A person, whose arms once encircled me so magnificently and totally, I thought nothing could be so perfect, so complete. And yet the years have proven me so dismally shortsighted. For this was a person whose arms—and by extension, my arms—became an ever-widening circle to embrace children, who by an unseen—yet felt—divine power and our own love we brought into the world. This person took on the challenge of the most important job married people have—outside of loving each other—and proved that our partnership was not limited to two, that there was so much more of each of us that could be summoned. That only by sharing our love so recklessly, so daily, so unsurely would we truly understand the very meaning of our lives on earth.

And yet, a person who can shut the world out, whose arms form once again that smaller, selfish circle that has no room for another being. Only me.

5. . . . *Someone who knows and allows my secrets*
   . . . Yet breaks down the barriers.

This is a most delicate balance, but it is at the very core of the mystery and the beauty of marriage. For being married means there will be a person who knows the deepest parts of me, the best and worst of me, and allows me to—well—be. Yet, this can never be a case of mutual avoidance, standoff. No. I like being married because here is a person who will fearlessly break through my defenses to rescue me from myself or at times boldly confront me with attitudes or actions that simply cannot continue. So, someone who respects my boundaries but is willing to breach them. A person who at once envelops me, yet gives me room to breathe. In the end, a person who shares and experiences that deepest part of me—but not all of me, for there is a part that only we ourselves and God will ever know.

6. . . . Someone to regard the world with.

A person with whom, day after day, I can look upon the world and share my thoughts as I share hers. This passing world, the majesty and craziness of the days we spend together. Someone who I can laugh and cry with about what is happening to us, our family, our world. Only marriage provides that continuing and shared vantage point, a dual ringside seat on life where, as the years go by, the understanding takes on new depth, where sometimes no words need to be spoken to completely understand what another person is thinking. This is magical, ethereal, profound . . . and wonderfully daily and ordinary.

7. . . . Someone to be truly committed to.

Marriage is for life—we hope—but there must be a reason for such a deep and lasting relationship. Marriage calls for a profound level of intimacy, but such intimacy cannot be achieved unless a spouse is a person who is at once fascinating, complex, changing, deep enough, so much so that we are constantly stretching, reaching. One of the wonders of being married is finding a partner—and I say this not with any arrogance–who is worthy of our commitment. Someone worth sacrificing for. Someone worth taking the time to understand. A marathon to be run, a mountain to be climbed— these are great and visible challenges. But the commitment of one person to another in marriage—this is truly a lifetime's effort, worth and worthy of our best efforts.

8. . . . Someone whom I can honestly call "friend."

Lover? Yes. Partner? Yes. But to call my wife a friend is the highest honor I can pay her. For marriage is truly the most intimate relationship, a crucible of daily events repeated again and again; a roller coaster of human emotions. And to have a true friend at my side, on the other end of a phone, in

"To call my wife a friend is the highest honor I can pay her."

the bathroom, walking down the beach—this is to have one of the most profound gifts that anyone can have. For this friend to whom I am married is bonded to me in a way no other being ever will be. And this friend to whom I am married both knows me better and has lived with me longer than any other person.

9. . . . *Someone who understands that marriage is holy, a sacrament.*

This is the crucial, transcendent dimension of married life. For our life together, the life that may embrace children, is, to my mind, somehow incomplete without the realization that what we are about is a holy work. A work designed and inspired and supported by a Divine Presence. That Divine Presence may have different names to different married couples; that is of little importance. What is important is the acknowledgment that this Divine Presence—God to me—is father, friend, sustainer and without Him we have already divorced . . . divorced ourselves from the divine source of life and love. I like being married–and probably this is why I chose the woman I did—so that I can talk to God in a new and more complete way to her. I can search for God, with her. My needs are greater. So are His blessings for both of us and this family.

10. . . . *Someone who loves me and allows me to love them.*

This word "love" is so casually tossed around, but only when I married did I begin to understand its complexity, its benefits, the pain it sometimes exacts. "Harsh and dreadful" says Dostoyevsky about love not in theory but in practice. I like being married, of course, to experience the realization of someone's love. But, as importantly, to have a person who is vulnerable enough to allow my love to matter—above all the other loves, real or imagined—in this world. What is better, feeling loved or loving? We need not answer that, but just to know that this circle of being loved and loving is the greatest power we experience in our life. It lasts, over years and trials. It grows deeper. It understands. It forgives. It becomes more important day by day. For it is far easier—and ultimately less satisfying—to love everyone shallowly. Marriage to that some*one* focuses us, bringing forth possibilities we might never have known.

Paul Wilkes, an award-winning journalist and author, lives with his wife, Tracy, and their two sons in Wilmington, North Carolina. Paul and Tracy have been married since 1982.

∽∞∾

No matter what else I do, asking Laura to marry me was the best decision of my life.
—George W. Bush, married to Laura
since 1977

Really, when one is so happy and blessed in one's home life as I am, politics must take second place.
—Queen Victoria

I like being married because I enjoy sharing a house with the person I'm in love with. Every so often I look up and see him doing ordinary things, and I get that wonderful tingle.
—Yvonne Yax
Greenwich, Connecticut

One of the best things about love is just recognizing a man's step when he climbs the stairs.
—Colette

It is good everywhere,
but home is better.

—Yiddish proverb

Marriage does for each other. I love it when John thinks of me, waits on me, waits for me, and watches out for me. I'm sure he loves it when I do the same for him. We do it for each other and miraculously get back what we give.

—Paula Dore
Glenview, Illinois

Even though I'm not Superman, Paula's love, respect, and enthusiasm makes me feel that I am.

—John Dore
Glenview, Illinois

The day I discovered the wonder of love was not on my wedding day when, wide-eyed and hopeful, I took the hand of my young bridegroom and stepped out of the chapel.

It was the day many years later when I pulled on an old and favorite pair of pants and found to my dismay that the ten pounds I thought I had lost had simply shifted south and stuck.

When Gary came home that night, he found me weeping before the mirror over my too-tight pants—and the new sags and wrinkles that I had discovered on my face. To his credit, my husband didn't laugh. He took me into his arms and assured me that, yes, he would love me even if the pouches under my eyes sagged down to my chin and the bulges at my hips migrated to my knees.

"You look the same as you always did—beautiful," he said. And to prove it, he drove me to the ice-cream store and bought me a frozen yogurt—low calorie, of course. With fresh strawberries. Just the way I like it.

—Linda Ching Sledge
Pleasantville, New York

The longer Carol and I have been married, the more I notice that a curious division of labor has set in. Something more basic than who washes the dishes, cooks the meals, or balances the checkbook. For instance, I've always been terrible at remembering names, but Carol's a genius at it, so now I count on her when we meet new people. On the other hand, she can't remember numbers and dates for the life of her. "When was World War II over?" she asks as she looks up from the newspaper, which is just the sort of date that seems to stick in my head.

What I notice as she takes over more and more names and I do more numbers is that I would be lost without her. A cynic might point out that this is the weakness of marriage. Spouses give up part of themselves by depending on each other. But I find it liberating. I don't have to know and do everything for myself. Interdependence seems to bring freedom.

—Rick Hamlin
New York, New York

Cynics refer to marriage as "the old ball and chain." For us marriage is freeing and enabling. When we look into each other's eyes we see all our strengths and possibilities. We teach each other to accept and love ourselves, and we are motivated to be the best that we can be instead of accepting our least. We transform each other from the ordinary to the extraordinary.

So for us marriage means freedom to be who we really are and assurance that we will accept and love each other no matter what. It enables us to reach for the stars and discover what we are meant to be without fear or ridicule or rejection.

—Leroy and Kathy Moore
Annapolis, Maryland

⚭

Forty Things Married Couples Like Best about Being Married

COMPILED BY SUE AND TOM JOHNSON (FROM NATIONAL MARRIAGE ENCOUNTER COUPLES THROUGHOUT THE UNITED STATES)

1. Sharing the good of God with your best friend
2. Overcoming life's difficulties together
3. Knowing there is someone to come home to after working all day

4. Knowing that should better turn to worse you will never leave each other

5. Not being alone when you're sick or in the hospital

6. The silly little jokes only you know

7. Someone to help you see light when everything seems dark

8. The children you've been blessed with

9. The grandchildren that your children have blessed you with

10. All the gifts that God blesses you with all the time

11. Hugs in good times and bad

12. Cuddling in front of a fire

13. Powerful feelings of gratitude

14. The ability to share openly and completely when you're troubled, or in trouble

15. Someone to watch movies and television with

16. Someone to help you rake leaves or plant flowers

17. Soft kisses when you least expect them

18. Praying together

19. Walking together

20. Traveling together

21. Laughing together

22. Quiet times together

23. Encouragement to be the best you can be

24. Being loved unconditionally

25. The gift of being an example of a good marriage to your children

26. The freedom to be just "yourself"

27. The opportunity to learn and practice generosity

28. Someone who wants to get an ice-cream cone at the same time you do

29. Laughter

30. Friends

31. Receiving good example, and giving it without knowing it

32. Sexual intimacy

33. Pillow talk

34. Kissing and making up

35. Your spouse's acceptance of your family

36. A warm hand to hold in church

37. Marriage Encounter weekends

38. Dancing
39. Babies
40. Anniversaries

Tom and Sue Johnson of Waterford, Wisconsin, are the Executive Couple for National Marriage Encounter, overseeing affiliates throughout the United States. They have been married since 1969.

∞

I like being married. I liked being single too. It was carefree, spontaneous, and adventurous. The downside was that all of the good stuff I did ended up with just *me*, having fun but ultimately only with and for *me*. I wanted someone to share with. I needed someone to share with.

Then, when I got married and had someone to share with, I began to look back on single life through rose-colored glasses of remembrance. Had I given my right to be *me* in exchange for an opportunity to experience *us*? Soon I knew: I had given nothing up. Liz and I didn't know for sure what *us* was going to be like, but we did know that we loved each other and wanted to create a loving *us*, and all we had to build on was the *she* and *me* we started with.

As it turns out, her *she* and my *me* are more alike than we ever knew. They *both* are fun and carefree and spontaneous and adventurous. There is no downside. And at the center of and at the end of our adventures together, there is now she and me as *us*. And that's why I like being married.

—Nick DiFranco
Red Bank, New Jersey

Marriage moves us from ego to we-go. The single self shifts from me first to the sacred union of *us*. Spiritual values such as love, honesty, respect, fidelity, and dependability form the engine of a good marriage. Little kindnesses are the oil. Without the oil, it will grind. With it, it glides.

—Paula Dore
Glenview, Illinois

After fifty-four years of being together, to say we like being married is a peculiar understatement. Much has happened in the years gone by—good and not so good—but nothing in my life would have any rationale without my wife and the family structure we have built together. Marriage sometimes sounds like a corporation. I like to think of it as *us,* and the openness, trust, intimacy, and compassion (the real stuff of love) that we have shared these many years. I can't contemplate an alternative to the life I've had, in large part to Ellie, our three children, their spouses, and our six grandchildren.

—Theodore Isaac Rubin
New York, New York

My grandparents defied every relationship rule or model I have ever heard about. They probably exchanged no more than 25 words a week. But they spoke about each other whenever they had the chance: He told everybody that she was crazy as a "peach orchard borer"; she told people he was so old that she had to remind him to breathe. Yet no matter where they were or what they were doing, they managed to be physically very close and in most cases actually touching. They had a huge dinner table in a giant old house, and they would sit at one little corner of the table—just the two of them—scrunched up together. They were married 68 years when my grandfather passed away.

—Dr. Phil McGraw,
married to Robin since 1978

Share with me your laughter.
Share with me your tears,
Your hopes and aspirations,
Your heartaches and your fears.
Share with me any disappointment
That makes your world stop,
Any big or small accomplishment
I can shout from a mountaintop.
Share with me that special song
That makes everything alright.

*Share with me a
good morning kiss
After a fantastic
night.
Share with me the
good and bad
Is all I ask of you,
Because to share a life
is the reason
behind
My promise of "I Do."*

The Cupps bubble with happiness on their wedding day.

—Quentin and Krissy Cupp
Annapolis, Maryland

I like being married because I married somebody better than me. In the 37 years Barbara and I have been together, I've become a different and better person.

—Herman Jacobi
Jackson, Mississippi

I am not good alone. I worry. I do not laugh easily. I am selfish. I am critical. I am many things that I do not like and do not want to be.

With Julie, I laugh and tease. My problems shrink, my shared worries dissipate. She gives me a direction for my love, for my emotions, and I am more selfless because I have been given someone to cherish, to love, to protect.

With the girl who first sought me out at 16, I learned that laughter is natural and fun; that sharing is a wonderful experience. Sharing dreams, small triumphs, disappointments, the highs, the lows, the joys, the sorrows, the contentment of life with one so loved. All this and undemanding love. How could it be better?

Without the warmth, the understanding, the caring, I would be a very different person—less open, more easily hurt, and far less confident in who I am.

I like being married. Every one of the 60 years has been better than the last one. Seems impossible since I thought the first year was wonderful, happy, and bright. Being married put me on a joyous new path with rich rewards all along the way including children, grandchildren, and a great-grandchild. All of this is encased in a cocoon of love that has made for unalloyed happiness, growth, and acceptance.

—Win Firman
Amherst, Massachusetts

Until you're a hundred,
Until I'm ninety-nine,
Together
Until white hair grows.

—Japanese folk song

INTERLUDE

How Do I Love Thee?

BY ELIZABETH BARRETT BROWNING

How do I love thee? Let me count the ways.
I love thee to the depth and breadth and height
My soul can reach, when feeling out of sight
For the ends of Being and ideal Grace.
I love thee to the level of everyday's
Most quiet need, by sun and candle-light.
I love thee freely, as men strive for Right;
I love thee purely, as they turn from Praise.
I love thee with the passion to put use
In my old griefs, and with my childhood's faith.
I love thee with a love I seemed to lose
With my lost saints,—I love thee with the breath,
Smiles, tears, of all my life!—and, if God choose,
I shall but love thee better after death.

Chapter Three

IT'S BEEN AROUND A LONG TIME

♡ *We are all born for love.*
— *Disraeli*

In the Beginning . . .

The Lord God said, "It is not good that the man should be alone."
So the Lord God caused a deep sleep to fall upon the man, and he
slept; and then he took one of his ribs and closed up its place with

flesh. And the rib that the Lord God had taken from the man he made into a woman and brought her to the man. Then the man said,

> *"This at last is bone of my bones*
> *and flesh of my flesh;*
> *this one shall be called Woman,*
> *for out of Man this one was taken."*

Therefore a man leaves his father and his mother and clings to his wife, and they become one flesh.

—Genesis 2:18, 21–24

Jacob loved Rachel; so he said to Laban, "I will serve you seven years for your younger daughter Rachel." So Jacob served seven years for Rachel, and they seemed to him but a few days because of the love he had for her.

—Genesis 29:18, 20

Happy is the husband of a good wife;
the number of his days will be doubled.
A loyal wife brings joy to her husband,
and he will complete his years in peace.
A good wife is a great blessing;
she will be granted among the blessings of the man who fears the Lord.
Whether rich or poor, his heart is content,
and at all times his face is cheerful.

—Sirach 26:1–4

∝⊗ↄ

Ancient Love

BY HOMER

Now from his breast into his eyes the ache
of longing mounted, and he wept at last,
his dear wife, clear and faithful, in his arms,

longed for
as the sunwarmed earth is longed for by a swimmer
spent in rough water where his ship went down
under Poseidon's blows, gale winds and tons of sea.
Few men can keep alive through a big surf
to crawl, clotted with brine, on kindly beaches
in joy, in joy, knowing the abyss behind:
and so she too rejoiced, her gaze upon her husband,
her white arms round him pressed as though forever. . . .
So they came
into that bed so steadfast, loved of old,
opening glad arms to one another.
Telémakhos by now had hushed the dancing,
hushed the women. In the darkened hall
he and the cowherd and the swineherd slept.
The royal pair mingled in love again
and afterward lay revelling in stories:
hers of the siege her beauty stood at home
from the arrogant suitors, crowding on her sight,
and how they fed their courtship on his cattle,
oxen and fat sheep, and drank up rivers
of wine out of the vats.
Odysseus told
of what hard blows he had dealt out to others
and what blows he had taken—all that story.
She could not close her eyes till all was told.
                    —The Odyssey

And on the shield he fashioned of men two cities fair;
And in the first they weddings make, and marriage feasts prepare;
And brides from forth their chamber they lead with torches bright
Along the streets and Hymen call:
"Hymen, O Hymen," should they all, and nuptial songs recite.
The youngsters dance in measure, with sound of harp and flute;
The women standing at their doors look on amazed and mute.
                    —The Iliad

So ancient is the desire of one another which is implanted in us, re-uniting our original nature, seeking to make one of two, and to heal the state of man. Each of us when separated, having one side only, like a flat fish, is but the tally-half of a man, and he is always looking for his other half.

—Plato

To the eternal memory of Blandina Martiola, a most faultless girl, who lived eighteen years, nine months, five days. Pompeius Catussa, a Sequanian citizen, a plasterer, dedicated this to his wife, who was incomparable and very kind to him, who lived with him for five years, six months, eighteen days without any shadow of a fault, this memorial which he has erected in his lifetime for himself and his wife and which he consecrated while it was still under con-struction. You who read this, go bathe in the baths of Apollo, as I used to do with my wife. I wish I still could.

—An epitaph from Roman France

❧

Classic Love

BY GEOFFREY CHAUCER AND WILLIAM SHAKESPEARE

Virginity is indeed a great perfection,
And married continence, for God's dilection,
But Christ, who of perfection is the well,
Bade not that everyone should go and sell
All that he had and give it to the poor
To follow in His footsteps, that is sure.
He spoke to those that would live perfectly,
And by your leave, my lords, that's not for me.
I will bestow the flower of life, the honey,
Upon the acts and fruit of matrimony.

—Geoffrey Chaucer

Let me not to the marriage of true minds
Admit impediments. Love is not love
Which alters when it alteration finds,
Or bends with the remover to remove:
O, no! it is an ever-fixed mark,
That looks on tempests and is never shaken;
It is the star to every wandering bark,
Whose worth's unknown, although his height be taken.
Love's not Time's fool, though rosy lips and cheeks
Within his bending sickle's compass come;
Love alters not with his brief hours and weeks,
But bears it out even to the edge of doom.
   If this is error, and upon me prov'd,
   I never writ, nor no man ever lov'd.

—William Shakespeare

⸎

Blest Day That I Made Her My Own

BY BENJAMIN FRANKLIN

Of their Cloes and Phillisses poets may prate
   I sing my plain Country Joan
Now twelve years my wife, still the joy of my life
   Blest day that I made her my own,
     My dear friends
   Blest day that I made her my own.
Not a word of her face, her shape, or her eyes,
   Of flames or of darts shall you hear;
Tho' I beauty admire 'tis virtue I prize,
   That fades not in seventy years,
     My dear friends
In health a companion delightful and dear,
   Still easy, engaging, and free,
In sickness no less than the faithfulest nurse

As tender as tender can be,
    My dear friends
Am I laden with care, she takes off a large share,
    That the burden ne'er makes me to reel,
Does good fortune arrive, the joy of my wife,
    Quite doubles the pleasures I feel,
        My dear friends
Some faults we have all, and so many my Joan,
    But then they're exceedingly small;
And now I'm us'd to 'em, they're just like my own,
    I scarcely can see 'em at all,
        My dear friends
    I scarcely can see 'em at all.
Were the fairest young princess, with million in purse
    To be had in exchange for my Joan,
She could not be a better wife, mought be a worse,
    So I'd stick to my Joggy alone
        My dear friends
I'd cling to my lovely ould Joan.

Benjamin Franklin, one of America's founding fathers, was married to Deborah from 1730 to 1790.

⌒∞⌒

Dearest Friend,

I have spent the 3 days past almost entirely with you. The weather has been stormy, I have had little company, and I have amused my self in my closet reading over the Letters I have received from you since I have been here. . . .

I have amused myself in reading and thinking of my absent Friend, sometimes with a mixture of pain, sometimes with pleasure, sometimes anticipating a joyful and happy meeting, whilst my Heart would bound and palpitate with the pleasing Idea, and with the purest affection I have held you to my Bosom till my whole Soul has dissolved in Tenderness and my pen fallen from my Hand.

How often do I reflect with pleasure that I hold in possession a Heart Equally warm with my own, and full as Susceptable [*sic*] of the Tenderest impressions, and Who even now whilst he is reading here, feels all I describe. . . .

I wish for peace and tranquility. All my desires and all my ambition is to be Esteemed and Loved by my Partner, to join with him in the Education and instruction of our Little ones, to set under our own vines in Peace, Liberty and Safety.

Adieu my Dearest Friend, soon, soon return to your most affectionate
Portia [Abigail Adams]

Not one day has passed that I have not loved you, not one night that I have not clasped you in my arms. I have not drunk so much as a cup of tea without cursing the call of glory and ambition which have wrenched me from you who are my life, my soul. In the midst of military affairs, at the head of my troops, in my inspections of the camps, my adorable Josephine holds undisputed sway over my heart, possesses my mind, engrosses my thoughts.

—Napoleon Bonaparte

I never, never spent such an evening!!! My dearest dearest dear Albert sat on a footstool by my side, and his excessive love and affection gave me feelings of heavenly love and happiness, I never could have hoped to have felt before!—really how can I ever be thankful enough to have such a Husband!

—Queen Victoria

We do not live in a world of small intrigues, but of serious and important affairs. I could not conceive myself forming any other attachment than that to which I have fastened the happiness of my life here below. . . . I do not love and will never love any woman in the world but you, and my chief desire is to link myself to you week by week by bonds which shall ever become more intimate and profound.

Beloved I kiss your memory—Your sweetness and beauty have cast a glory upon my life. You will find me always Your
loving and devoted husband
W [Winston Churchill]

I can't help wanting to talk to my sweetheart and my baby every night. I'm a damn fool I guess because I could never get excited or worked up about gals or women. I only had one sweetheart from the time I was six. I saw her in Sunday School at the Presbyterian Church in Independence when my mother took me there at that age and afterwards in the 5th grade at the Ott School in Independence when her Aunt Nannie was our teacher and she sat behind me. She sat behind me in the sixth, seventh and High School grades and I thought she was the most beautiful and the sweetest person on earth—and I'm still of that opinion after twenty-six years of being married to her. I'm old fashioned, I guess. But it's a happy state to labor under in this terrible job I fell heir to on April 12, '45.
—Harry S. Truman

We're too old to be single. Why should we both be married instead of sitting through the long winter evenings by our solitary firesides? Why shouldn't we make one fireside of it?

Come, let's be a comfortable couple, and take care of each other! How glad we shall be, that we have somebody we are fond of always, to talk to and sit with.

Let's be a comfortable couple. Now do, my dear!
—Charles Dickens

⌘

Jimmy's Picture
BY ROSALYNN CARTER

[1944] was the year I fell in love with Jimmy's picture.

Jimmy's sister, Ruth, was still in high school in Plains, and we continued to spend a lot of time together. I couldn't keep my eyes off the photograph of her idolized, older brother pinned up on her bedroom wall. I thought he was the most handsome man I had ever seen. I had known him as long as I could remember, the way everyone in a small town knows everyone else, but he was three years older than I and had been away at school for four years. I don't remember ever having said a word to him except when we bought ice cream cones from him one summer in the old bank building on the main street in town. He seemed so glamorous and out of reach.

Plotting a fantasy romance with him became a great game between Ruth and me. Whenever he was home at Christmas or on summer leave, she would call me to come to see her—and him. Every time she called I panicked. After looking at his picture so much and becoming so attached to it, I didn't know whether I could face the real Jimmy or not. And if I saw him in person, I didn't know whether I could say a single word to him. During the summer of 1945, Ruth and I kept trying to arrange a time for me to appear at their house when he was at home, but each time he had plans to be somewhere else. In a way it was a relief. I knew this was the person I would fall in love with, the person I wanted to have fall in love with me, but I never thought it would happen.

That summer, just before his leave was over, Ruth called. She and Jimmy were going to the Pond House for a picnic and to clean up the yard and would like me to go with them. . . . I went, of course, with great excitement and anticipation.

This time Jimmy paid attention to me, teasing me all day about everything, especially about the way I made my sandwich, with salad dressing instead of mayonnaise, and with the pieces of bread not matching. But I didn't mind. While we swept the house and raked the yards I discovered I could talk, actually talk, to him. I'd always been shy and quiet, and I was worried that I'd be speechless. But I wasn't. We had a very good time, although I was sure he was looking at me that day as much younger, as the age of his little sister Ruth. And when they took me home after lunch, I thought, That's that.

Later in the afternoon I went to a youth meeting at the church. It was a beautiful evening, and as I was standing outside with friends, suddenly a car drove up—and Jimmy got out. I couldn't believe it when he walked over and asked if I'd like to go to a movie with Ruth and her boyfriend—and him! While everyone watched, I left the church, forgot about the youth meeting altogether, and went off with Jimmy Carter. He was twenty. I was seventeen.

I have no idea what movie we saw that night. My mind was somewhere else. After dreaming about him for so long, I was actually with him, and it couldn't have been more wonderful. We rode in the rumble seat of the car, the moon was full in the sky, conversation came easy, and I was in love with a real person now, not just a photograph. And on the way home, he kissed me! I couldn't believe it happened. I had never let any boy kiss me on a first date. My mother told me she hadn't even held hands with Daddy until they were engaged! But I was completely swept off my feet.

Rosalynn Carter, former First Lady of the United States and author of *First Lady from Plains,* has been married to Jimmy since 1946.

⸙

And when will there be an end of marrying? I suppose, when there is an end of living!
                    —Tertullian

Falling in Love

BY MARIANNE WILLIAMSON

Falling in love has been getting a bad rap recently. Supposedly more sophisticated types suggest that falling in love is an illusion, a state of non-reality because it is based on failure to see the love object as a "real" human being. According to this view, "real" love sets in only at the end of infatuation. A beautiful smile or dreams of greatness, for instance, are not considered as *real* as one's tendency to squeeze the toothpaste from the top of the tube.

From an illumined perspective, falling in love is not neurotic but rather one of the few genuinely non-neurotic things we do on this earth. Falling in love is an effort to retrieve Paradise, that dimension of bliss where no one is blamed for anything and everyone is fully appreciated for who they are. When we fall in love, we drop for however brief a time our tendency to judge. We suspend our disbelief and eschew our faithlessness in another human being.

What usually happens after that is not that we finally wake up to reality. What tends to happen after that is that we *fall asleep* to reality. We cannot wake up to our brother's imperfections, because the perception of imperfection is itself a nonawakened state. Our spiritual perfection is not altered by our imperfect personalities. Seeing perfection is seeing the light. Falling in love is not an illusion, as much as falling *out* of love is a fall from grace.

What we see when we fall in love is not illusion but truth. We want to fall in love because we want so much to return to God. Of course we want to escape this darkened world. We want desperately to go home to a place where all of us can see how beautiful we are.

Some people say that falling in love is a state of denial. It is, actually. In love, we are in a *positive* denial: a denial of darkness. What then occurs is that we start to believe the serpent's lies—we begin to see good and evil: "I like him, but he doesn't make enough money" or "I like her, but she's too high maintenance." Spirit has celebrated how wonderful they are; now the negative mind gets to celebrate how *guilty* they are. Guilt is the ego's orgasm.

Most people do not have the personality structure to hold on to the strength it takes to love without judgment. And so love's magic dies, casting Adam and Eve out of Paradise.

As our minds are illumined, we become better at romance because we become better at being human. We become better at forgiveness and support and love. The enlightened world will not be one in which no one ever falls in love. The enlightened world will be one in which everyone is in love with everyone all the time. There will be no judgment, therefore, no blocks to the awareness of love. We will see each other as God created us: as the perfect, loving and lovable people we really are at our core. The purpose of romantic love is to jump start our enlightenment.

Chapter Four

ISN'T IT ROMANTIC?

*What if
the Hokey Pokey
really is...
what it's all about?*

I buy the wild little nightie every now and then to surprise him. I'll leave him a love note, or practice my golf swing naked.
—Cheryl Ladd,
married to Brian Russell since 1981

On the morning of Valentine's Day, he surprised me with a trail of candles and gardenias on our floor that led to an arrangement of tulips. You have to work to create that.

—Jenna Elfman,
married to Bodhi Elfman
since 1995

She just has to smile and I get kind of melty. She showers me with kisses in the morning. Sometimes I can't get out of bed until she gives me 30 or 40 kisses.

—Bodhi Elfman

I leave notes on his pillow with hearts on them. If we're going to be apart, I'll leave him a little something to let him know I'm thinking of him and to make him smile.

—Mariel Hemingway, married to
Steve Crisman since 1984

To keep the spice in our marriage, we play golf. I argue with him and joke that I need to work on my game so I can beat him. Romantic for us is normal life—cooking and buying groceries. I like to be at home with Rene. He knows me by heart.

—Celine Dion,
married to René Angélil since 1994

He says, "I love you, baby," and takes my face in his hands. It's those little personal moments between a couple.

—Natasha Richardson, married to
Liam Neeson since 1994

I knew it had happened: I had fallen in love. I wanted to be Camille's husband. I wondered if I would ever be able to tell her about it. . . .

How intoxicating it was to be in love, to be making this mad trip south to Camille! My future was enchanting, my past a series of fading flops.

My love life had left me with so many forgettable memories; but improved memories lay ahead with Camille, who promised infinitely more than a passing press or a sometime thigh or a loss of circulation. As I drove past Elizabeth, New Jersey (had I ever gone out with *her*?), I found myself singing:

Now I'm not crying in the chapel
Or even frowning near a priest.
Instead I'm smiling on the turnpike
In spite of driving half the East.

It was during one of those interstate lunches that I asked Camille to marry me.

"I'd love to marry you," she replied.

Suddenly I knew that I was one of God's favorites.

—Bill Cosby, married to Camille since 1964

✺

Blind Date

BY COLIN POWELL

One November day in 1961 I was stretched out in my room at the bachelor officers' quarters at Fort Devens when a friend, Michael Heningburg, popped in to ask me for a buddy-in-a-pinch favor. Mike had met a girl in Boston, Jackie Fields, and had flipped over her. "I'm asking you to go into town with me to pick off her roommate," he pleaded.

"A blind date?" I asked warily. Mike nodded. I had never been on a blind date. The odds of success seemed better in the numbers racket. Yet, my relationship with my girlfriend in New York had not survived the sixteen-month separation, and I was at loose ends. I had plenty of friends at Devens. But as far as romance, I was on the inactive list. "Okay, Mike," I said. "I'll run interference for you."

We drove to the Back Bay section of Boston to pick up the girls at 372 Marlborough Street. We were buzzed into a one-bedroom apartment on the ground floor in the rear of a brownstone. Jackie Fields greeted us, and a few minutes later, the other girl emerged. "This is my roommate, Alma Johnson," Jackie said.

She was fair-skinned, with light brown hair and a lovely figure. I was mesmerized by a pair of luminous eyes, an unusual shade of green. Miss Johnson moved gracefully and spoke graciously, with a soft Southern accent. This blind date might just work out.

Long afterward, Alma gave me her version of that first meeting. "I had had an argument with my roommate for getting me involved," she told me. "I do not go on blind dates," Alma had told Jackie. "And I definitely don't go on blind dates with soldiers. How do I know who's going to walk through that door?" Alma had worked off her annoyance by dressing up weirdly and piling on makeup to put off the unknown suitor when he arrived. But when she peeked into the room, she was surprised, she said, to see a shy, almost baby-faced guy, his cheeks rosy from the cold. She was used to dating men four or five years older. "You looked like a little lost twelve-year-old," she later told me. She had then disappeared into the bathroom to change her clothes, redo her face, and unvamp herself.

We took the girls out to a club in the Dorchester section. We had a few drinks, listened to music, and talked. After almost exclusive exposure to girls with New Yawky voices, I was much taken by this soft-spoken Southerner. And Alma did talk, most of the evening, while I listened entranced. At one point, she put a question to me natural enough in that era of compulsory military service: How much time did I have left in the Army? Young men she knew went into the service and got out as soon as possible; they could practically tell you how many minutes they still had to serve. I was not getting out, I told her; I was a career military. She looked at me as if I were an exotic specimen.

Finally, the most enjoyable night I had had in ages came to an end and Mike and I drove back to Fort Devens. I called Alma the next day and asked her out again.

We began to see each other regularly, and the more I saw, the more I liked.

Colin Powell, United States Secretary of State, has been married to Alma since 1962.

In Monaco, I told her that I loved her.

We were dressing for dinner in our hotel room, when suddenly we both grew quiet. Up to that moment, it had all been undercurrents. But as I watched her from across the room, I knew exactly what I was feeling, the tangled twisted strands of love. Only Kik was clear to me. Other than her, I was living in a state of utter confusion; I didn't know if I was going to live or die, and if I did live, I had no idea what I would do with my life. I didn't know what I wanted out of cycling anymore. I didn't know whether I wanted to ride, or retire, or go to college, or become a stockbroker. But I loved Kik.

If you ever hope to meet someone and fall in love, it should happen just as it did for us, blissfully, perfectly. Our relationship tended to be unspoken, a matter of a lot of deep, intense gazing, and a complex strum of emotions.

—Lance Armstrong,
married to Kristin
since 1998

When we met, I was immediately drawn to him. He was very impressive—a handsome, proud, and serious man with a warm smile and a pigeon-toed walk.

—Rachel Robinson, married to Jackie
from 1946 until his death in 1972

I didn't think anything could come into my life that would be more vital to me than my sports career. I believed that until Ray Bartlett, my best friend at UCLA, introduced me to Rachel Isum. . . . I was immediately attracted to Rachel's looks and charm, but as in many love stories, I didn't have the slightest idea I was meeting a young lady who would become the most important person in my life.

—Jackie Robinson

I can't speak for George Bush, but I fell madly in love.

—Barbara Bush,
married to George
since 1945

She was beautiful. I asked her to dance, and here we are fifty-four years later.

—George Bush

We met at a party that was held after my high school senior prom. She had a date with someone else. But I was smitten. I called her up the next day and asked her if she would go out with me on a date the following weekend.

—Al Gore, married to Tipper since 1970

⌘

Dear St. Valentine

I'm writing to you about a beautiful young lady who has been in this household for 24 years now—come March 4th.

I have a request to make of you but before doing so feel you should know more about her. For one thing she has 2 hearts—her own and mine. I'm not complaining. I gave her mine willingly and like it right where it is. Her name is Nancy but for some time now I've called her Mommie and don't believe I could change.

My request of you is—could you on this day whisper in her ear that someone loves her very much and more and more each day? Also tell her, this "someone" would run down like a dollar clock without her so she must always stay where she is.

Then tell her if she wants to know who that "someone" is to just turn her head to the left. I'll be across the room waiting to see if you told her. If you'll do this for me, I'll be happy knowing that she knows I love her with all my heart.

Thank you,
"Someone" [Ronald Reagan],
married to Nancy since 1952

In the fall of 1947, we were booked at the rodeo in Chicago. We were on our horses, in the chutes, waiting to be introduced, when Roy said, "Dale, what are you doing New Year's Eve?"

New Year's Eve was still months away. I had no plans.

Roy's face crinkled into that overpowering smile of his. His eyes sparkled. He reached into his pocket and pulled out a small box. Inside it was a gold ring set with a ruby. He reached down for my hand and slipped the ring on my finger. "Well, then," he said. "Why don't we get married?"

The drum roll sounded, the lights dimmed, Trigger reared up, and Roy Rogers galloped into the arena to the thunder of applause. I followed, on cue, and our horses took their position side by side in the spotlight in front of thousands of people. Before lifting the microphone to sing the National Anthem, I turned to look at Roy. He looked back at me, beaming with delight. The din of cheers made it impossible to speak. I formed the word "Yes" with my lips. He nodded, and we began to sing.

—Dale Evans, married to Roy Rogers
from 1947 until his death in 1998

At Neysa's studio, I picked up a glass of sherry to fit in and retreated to a secluded niche. About twenty minutes later, a good-looking fellow with curly brown hair and sparkling green eyes came over, maybe because he felt sorry for me sitting there all alone. He held out a small paper bag, "Wanna peanut?" he asked. "Thanks," I said. He poured a few in my hand and said, "I wish they were emeralds."

Well, I was bowled over. Right then and there I fell in love with Charles MacArthur, the most beautiful, most amusing, most amazing and dazzling man I had ever met.

—Helen Hayes, married to Charles
MacArthur from 1928 until his death
in 1956

At one point, Ossie stood up on stage and silently, slowly began tying his tie. At that moment, I distinctly remember feeling something like a bolt a lightning, an electrical charge, flash between us. Although I didn't move, I felt a physical jolt. . . . The whole thing made me think of the classical Cupid with his bow and arrow.

—Ruby Dee, married to Ossie Davis
since 1948

I loved Gracie, for whatever reason. That I was sure of. I hadn't fallen in love with Gracie's face, or her legs, or her bust, or her voice, or her timing. I fell in love with the whole package. But she did have great timing. And years later, when we were rich, I still loved her. And I still love her today. So whatever my reasons at first, it worked. It worked for a long, long time.

—George Burns, married to Gracie Allen
from 1926 until her death in 1964

Finding Shakira
BY MICHAEL CAINE

My friend Paul and I had been watching the same TV show for a while when the commercials came on. I was just about to reach for my broom pole and switch channels when something caught my attention. The ad was banging on about the quality of the beans in the coffee and on the screen a Brazilian girl was dancing around holding up maracas filled with beans. (Apparently the beans not only tasted good but sounded good as well.) The girl with the maracas was dancing

The face that launched a thousand heartbeats.
© TIMEPIX (TERRY SMITH)

49

in a long shot, but there was something about her that made me hope that there would be a close-up of her before the commercial ended; then, as if the director had read my mind, there it was—a close-up of the most beautiful girl I had ever seen. The effect on me was extraordinary. My heart started to pound and I grew very agitated. The palms of my hands, I noticed, were beginning to sweat and I suddenly found myself down on my knees in front of the set trying to get a closer look at this vision, only to be confronted with a close-shot of a Maxwell House coffee jar.

"What's the matter with you?" said a very puzzled Paul.

"That girl," I replied, hardly able to speak. "She's beautiful."

"I know," said Paul. "So what?"

"I want to meet her," I told him.

"How can you meet her? She's in Brazil," he said sensibly.

Paul came back in with the coffees. "Do you want to come to Brazil with me?" I asked him.

"To find that girl?"

"Yes," I said.

"Are you mad?" he said. "There are loads of beautiful girls in London."

"Not like this one," I replied maniacally.

Paul realized I was serious and agreed to come with me. "When?" he said with immediate practicality.

"Tomorrow or whenever the first plane goes," was my reply.

"I'm all for a trip to Brazil," he said, "so I don't want to put you off, but I think you're mad."

I thought about this for a moment and eventually came to the conclusion that he was right. I was mad—madly in love with a girl whom I did not know and might never find, but I knew what I was going to do first thing in the morning. I was going to phone Maxwell House and find out who had made the commercial for them.

We had eaten and the television was finished but I was too restless to go to bed yet so I suggested to Paul that we set off for a walk. It was now about half-past midnight and Paul knew very well what a walk meant at that time of night: a trip to Tramp, my favorite hangout, where my friends Johnny Gold and Oscar Lerman who owned the place were always good for a shoulder to cry on or an ear to listen to the troubles of the lovelorn. . . .

Above the din of the disco music I sat with Johnny and screamed my story of having at last found true love with a girl I had only seen on the television. Johnny listened sympathetically to my protestations and ordered a brandy for Paul and myself like a doctor dispensing placebos. He had heard it all many times before, though never from me. . . .

I was just about to leave when a guy I knew vaguely called Nigel Politzer came in and expressed surprise at seeing me sitting there with Paul and Johnny and no date. "I'm in love!" I told him.

"Oh yeah? Who with?" he asked, laughing at such a ridiculous statement.

"A girl I saw on television tonight," I replied without embarrassment, having by now had three or four brandies.

"I've been watching television all evening," Nigel replied. "Which show was she in?"

"She wasn't in a show. She was in a commercial for Maxwell House coffee," I said.

He roared with laughter and to my amazement said, "The one with the maracas?"

"Yes!" I replied, in wonder. "How on earth did you guess that?"

"I didn't guess," he replied. "I work for the company that made that commercial."

I couldn't believe my luck! Here was someone who could actually help me locate her. "Paul and I are going to Brazil tomorrow to find her. Do you know how we could contact her there?" I asked hopefully.

At this point Nigel went into hysterics. . . . "She's not in Brazil and she's not Brazilian. She's Indian and her name is Shakira Baksh."

Shakira Baksh, I thought. I had a name for her now. "Do you know where she lives?" I asked Nigel rather diffidently.

"Somewhere in the Fulham Road," he replied, which was about a mile from where we were sitting.

"Can you get her number?" I asked.

"Yes, the agency will have it."

"Will you do me a favor and phone her, and ask her permission to give me her number?" I knew it would not look good if he just gave it to me and I phoned out of the blue. Ladies, and that is what I rightly figured she was, don't like having their numbers passed round to strangers, and I didn't want to start off any relationship that might develop on the wrong foot. Nigel agreed and said that he would phone me the next day.

I strolled back to Grosvenor Square with Paul that night as happy as a kid just before Christmas, but still very nervous in case I did not get a present. It seemed like Fate to me, that I had gone to Tramp and met someone who already knew who she was, but things could still go wrong. Suppose she was married? I'd forgotten to ask Nigel that all-important question; she might be engaged or madly in love with someone! I started to panic as all these negative thoughts raced through my mind. It grew worse and worse. . . .

[Nigel] gave [her number] to me and I thanked him profusely and put the phone down. I stared at the number for a moment and then started to get nervous again. Now it was all up to me. I had to phone this woman and get her to come out with me. . . .

I decided to take the bull by the horns. "Would you have dinner with me some time?" I asked, in the least salacious tone I could muster, which actually came out sounding like a road-company Dracula.

"I'm busy for the next week," she said in a businesslike manner. "Could you call me again in about ten days' time?"

"Wonderful," I said, hiding my disappointment. "I look forward to seeing you." The phone went dead in my hand.

For the next ten days I walked around in a trance, unable to explain to myself, let alone others, what was happening to me. It was silly, I told myself. I had only seen this girl for a minute on television—what was going on? Nothing like this had ever happened to me before. Finally the time came to phone again. . . . She picked up the phone immediately and said yes, she would have dinner with me the next evening.

"Give me your address," I said, "and I'll pick you up at eight o'clock."

"No, you give me your address and I'll pick you up in my car," she said cautiously. . . .

"Anything you say," I replied obligingly, and gave her my address. . . .

There I was the next evening, bathed, shaved and stone-cold sober waiting for eight o'clock and my doorbell to ring. . . . I sat in an armchair in front of a television that I would not put on in case I could not hear the bell. After a while I could feel sweat trickling down underneath my arms. Panic set in. I rushed to the bathroom and sprayed the whole shirt liberally with after-shave and went back to waiting. I looked at my watch: it was right on eight o'clock. She would not be dead on time, I thought, and had just relaxed back for another couple of minutes' respite when the doorbell sent a deafening scream through my ears.

I rose slowly to my feet and strolled to the door, determined to present what I laughingly called my "man of the world" front, but somehow or other whatever holds up your knees had stopped functioning and my legs kept wobbling. I managed to get to the door and hang on to the handle where my knee-lock system quickly fell back into place and I looked through the peephole in my front door for my first sight in the flesh of this girl called Shakira. She looked gorgeous.

I opened the door slowly, revealing her face, millimeter by millimeter from left to right as it went until it was wide open and there was no barrier between us. There, smiling up at me, was the most beautiful woman that I had ever seen in my life.

"Hello, Michael," she said, extending her hand, which I took but did not shake. To shake this woman's hand would have been like an act of violence. I just held it and suddenly thought of something that the French say about love: "L'amour, c'est une question de peau." Love is a question of skin . . . there are only two types of touch. One is when you touch someone for the first time, and can tell that it is possible to fall in love with them but not necessarily so, and the other is a touch that tells you that you could never fall in love with this person.

The vibrations from Shakira throbbed through my hands and I knew that I had at least passed the first French test. Love *was* possible here, and somewhere deep in my heart I knew at that moment that it was also inevitable, at least on my part.

I suddenly realized that I had not spoken yet and I said, "Come in, Shakira," but no actual sound came out. I cleared my throat as surreptitiously as possible, and had another go, and this time I produced a sound which was not quite the seductive baritone for which I was aiming, but it at least got the message across and she came into my flat and into my life forever. It was as simple as that. I had heard of love at first sight but never really believed in it, yet here it was.

Michael Caine, Academy Award–winning actor, has been married to Shakira since 1973.

⌐∞⌐

I had been a fan of Gene Wilder's for many years, but the first time I saw him in person, my heart fluttered—I was hooked. It felt like my life went from black and white to Technicolor. Gene was funny and athletic and handsome, and he smelled good. I was bitten with love.

—Gilda Radner, married to Gene Wilder
from 1984 until her death in 1989

He's very romantic, and I love his mind. He's a great poet. I look at my parents who are just mad for each other. They've been married about 35 years, and they're as sexy and happy and talkative and crazy for each other as they've ever been. I wondered if I would ever be able to find what my parents have. I found it in David.

—Téa Leoni, married to David Duchovny
since 1997

I just could not believe that anyone could be so spiritual and beautiful at one and the same time. . . .

If I had not been smitten with love at first sight of Ruth Bell, I would certainly have been the exception. Many of the men at Wheaton thought she was stunning. Petite, vivacious, smart, talented, witty, stylish, amiable, and unattached. What more could a fellow ask for? . . .

Two things I felt sure of: first, that Ruth was bound to get married someday; and second, that I was the man she would marry.

—Billy Graham, married to Ruth Bell
Graham since 1943

$\propto\!\infty\!\sim$

Chasing Raisa
BY MIKHAIL GORBACHEV

My student years at [Moscow University] were very intense. Studies, lectures, and seminars took up at least twelve or fourteen hours daily—practically seven days a week.

I was reading one evening when two friends burst into my room. "Mishna," they said, "there's a wonderful girl! A new one. Let's go!"

"OK," I said, "you go ahead, I'll catch up with you later. . . ."

The boys left and I tried to continue studying. But curiosity finally got the better of me and I went to the [student] club. Little did I know that I went to meet my destiny.

From the entrance I noticed Yury Topilin, my roommate, tall and with his usual military stiffness, dancing with a girl I did not know. The music stopped. I went over to them and we were introduced. Raisa Titorenko was studying philosophy: the arts faculty was housed in the same university building as law, she lived in the same hostel on Stromynka Street, and I just cannot understand how I had not noticed her before.

From this day on, there began for me a period of torment and delight. My feeling at the time was that our first meeting had not impressed Raisa at all. She appeared calm and indifferent—judging by the look in her eyes. I tried to meet her again, and a friend once invited the girls from Raisa's room over to our room. We treated them to tea and spoke about everything with a certain exaltation, as always happens on such occasions. I wanted to "impress" her. I think I made a terrible fool of myself. She was reserved and the first to suggest breaking up the gathering. . . .

Time and again I tried to meet her and talk to her. But the weeks passed, a month, and then two months. It was only in December 1951 that an opportunity arose. One evening, having finished studying, I went over to the club. There was another meeting with artists, and the room was overcrowded. A short break was announced and I went down the aisle towards the stage, looking for some friends. I suddenly sensed rather than noticed that someone was looking at me. I greeted Raisa and said that I was looking for an empty seat.

"You can have mine, I am leaving," she answered, getting up, "it doesn't interest me that much."

I had the impression that she did not feel well and offered to accompany her. She did not object. It was early yet for us students, about ten, and I suggested taking a walk into the city. Raisa agreed, and a few minutes later we went down Stromynka Street to the Rusakov Club.

We had a long walk, discussing many subjects, mostly the imminent exams and other student business. The next day we met again, and soon we were spending all our free time together. The rest of my life somehow faded into the background. I even neglected my studies, although I passed the tests and the exams.

But one winter day, something unexpected happened. We met as usual after lectures in the Moscow University courtyard on Mokhavaya Street. We decided to walk back to the hostel on Stromynka Street, but Raya kept silent most of the way and answered my questions reluctantly. I sensed that something was wrong and asked her outright what it was. She unexpectedly said: "We shouldn't meet any more. I was happy all this time. I have come back to life. I broke with a man I trusted and it was a shattering blow to me. I am grateful to you. But I won't be able to get over anything like that should it happen again. Let's stop seeing each other now, before it's too late . . ."

We walked on for a while in silence. We were already close to Stromynka when I told Raya that I just could not satisfy her wish, that it would spell disaster for me. I thus confessed my feelings for her.

We entered the hostel. I saw Raya to her room and said before leaving her that I would be waiting for her at the same place, the square at Moscow State University, two days from now.

"We shouldn't meet any more," Raya insisted.

"I'll be waiting," I replied.

Two days later we met again.

And again, we spent all of our free time together. We strolled along the Moscow boulevards, exchanging our most intimate thoughts and discovering with wonder and joy all the things about each other that drew us closer.

In June 1952, we spent another sleepless night talking until dawn in the garden of our Stromynka Street hostel. Probably it was on that June night that we realized—we could not and should not part. Life was to prove that our choice was right.

Mikhail Gorbachev, former president of the Soviet Union, was married to Raisa from 1953 until her death in 1999.

⚭

I've never forgotten the first time I saw Peter. I know every inch of him now, but when I laid eyes on him that night I thought he stood six foot eleven—he just blotted out everything else in the room. . . .

I believe the word is smitten.

Peter's reaction to me was no less intense. Peter says it was what the French call a coup de foudre—a thunderbolt. We looked at each other and we fell in love. Just like that.

—Beverly Sills, married to Peter Greenough
since 1956

There was Anne, singing, in a beautiful white gown. She was singing "Married I Can Always Get," and I said to myself, "Gee, she's beautiful. I think I'll marry her." It was instant. I fell in love. As a matter of fact, I tripped over a cable and really fell in love. When she finished the song, I stood up and clapped, "Bravo!" I shouted. "Terrific!" Then I rushed up onto the stage. "Hi," I said, "I'm Mel Brooks." I was really a pushy kid. And I shook her hand, and she smiled and laughed. Three years later, I married her.

—Mel Brooks, married to Anne Bancroft
since 1964

I've been married to Mel Brooks 31 years. It's a case of opposites attract. He always amazes me, he's quite a remarkable man. The other night we were watching a baseball game. I was sewing, and he was engrossed in every play. When his team hit a home run, he was so excited he jumped up and

Springtime for Mel and Anne. © BETTMANN/CORBIS

down in happy hysterics. "What do you think of that?" he shouted over the roar of the stadium crowd. I looked up from sewing, studied the pitcher for a moment and said, "He's handsome." Disbelief filtered across his face, and he sat down, crossed his legs, picked up the paper and repeated, "Yes, dear, he is handsome." The sight of him imitating me made me laugh.

—Anne Bancroft

Paul and I loved each other. He told me he fell in love with me the first time we met, and that was so sweet of him to say, whether or not it was true. What really mattered so much to me was that he always would tell me that he was falling more and more in love with me as time went on.

—Linda McCartney, married to Paul from 1969 until her death in 1998

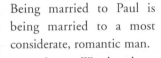

Being married to Paul is being married to a most considerate, romantic man.

—Joanne Woodward, married to Paul Newman since 1958

Joanne is one of the last of the great broads.

—Paul Newman

Nuptial Vows

I take thee to have and to hold, from this day forward, for better for worse, for richer for poorer, in sickness and in health, to love and to cherish, till death do us part, according to God's holy ordinance and thereto I give thee my troth.

With this ring, I thee wed, with my body I thee worship, and with all my worldly goods I thee endow.

—From the Book of Common Prayer

Groom: Be consecrated unto me as my wife according to the law of Moses and Israel. I will love, honor, and cherish you; I will protect and support you, and I will faithfully care for your needs, as prescribed by Jewish law and tradition.

Bride: In accepting the wedding ring, I pledge you all my love and devotion, and I take upon myself the fulfillment of all the duties incumbent upon a Jewish wife.

—From the ketubah

We have taken the seven steps. You have become mine forever. Yes, we have become partners. I have become yours. Hereafter, I cannot live without you. Do not live without me. Let us share the joys. We are word and meaning, united. You are thought and I am sound.

—From the Hindu marriage ritual of
"Seven Steps"

B*ride:* I offer you myself in marriage in accordance with the instructions of the holy Quran and the Holy Prophet, peace and blessing be upon him. I pledge in honesty and with sincerity to be for you an obedient and faithful wife.

Groom: I pledge in honesty and sincerity to be for you a faithful and helpful husband.

—From the Muslim wedding vows

Chapter   Five

WITH THIS RING . . .

To love another
is to touch the face
of God.

Victor Hugo

'Twas when the spousal time of May
Hangs all the hedge with bridal wreaths,
And air's so sweet the bosom gay
Gives thanks for every breath it breathes;
When like to like is gladly moved,
And each thing joins in Spring's refrain,
"Let those love now who never loved;
Let those who have loved love again."

—Coventry Patmore

☙

Favorite Wedding Readings

Then God said, "Let us make humankind in our image, according to our likeness; and let them have dominion over the fish of the sea, and over the birds of the air, and over the cattle, and over all the wild animals of the earth, and over every creeping thing that creeps upon the earth."

So God created humankind in his image,
In the image of God he created them;
Male and female he created them.

God blessed them, and God said to them, "Be fruitful and multiply, and fill the earth and subdue it; and have dominion over the fish of the sea and over the birds of the air and over every living thing that moves upon the earth." God saw everything that he had made, and indeed, it was very good.
—Genesis 1:26–28, 31

If I speak in the tongues of mortals and of angels, but do not have love, I am a noisy gong or a clanging cymbal. And if I have prophetic powers, and understand all mysteries and all knowledge, and if I have all faith, so as to remove mountains, but do not have love, I am nothing. If I give away all my possessions, and if I hand over my body so that I may boast, but do not have love, I gain nothing.

Love is patient; love is kind; love is not envious or boastful or arrogant or rude. It does not insist on its own way; it is not irritable or resentful; it does not rejoice in wrongdoing, but rejoices in the truth. It bears all things, believes all things, hopes all things, endures all things.

Love never ends. But as for prophecies, they will come to an end; as for tongues, they will cease; as for knowledge, it will come to an end. For we know only in part, and we prophesy only in part; but when the complete comes, the partial will come to an end.

When I was a child, I spoke like a child, I thought like a child, I reasoned like a child; when I became an adult, I put an end to childish ways. For now we see in a mirror, dimly, but then we will see face to face. Now I know only in part; then I will know fully, even as I have been fully known. And now faith, hope, and love abide, these three; and the greatest of these is love.

—1 Corinthians 13:1–13

As the Father has loved me, so I have loved you; abide in my love. If you keep my commandments, you will abide in my love, just as I have kept my Father's commandments and abide in his love. I have said these things to you so that my joy may be in you, and that your joy may be complete. This is my commandment, that you love one another as I have loved you.

—John 15:9–12

January 7, 1926, was the most important day in my life. That's when audiences discovered I had this big talent, and I stayed married to her for thirty-eight years. At that time getting married was so simple. At seven-thirty in the morning Gracie and I went to the Justice of the Peace; she said "I do"; I said "I do"; and we did.

—George Burns, married to Gracie Allen
from 1926 until her death in 1964

When Janet's brother John brought Janet up the aisle . . . that was one of the most stunning moments of my life. When I looked back and saw this beautiful woman, really radiant, really incredible, I think I went flush red. But more than just how she looked, I realized I was marrying someone I could spend this lifetime with and about nine others past that.

—Wayne Gretzky, married to Janet Jones
since 1988

cㅇ∞ɔ

Wedding Traditions from Around the World
BY DAPHNE ROSE KINGMA

*Every culture, country, and religious faith has its own unique wedding tra-
ditions. These not only reflect a particular cultural or religious outlook, but
also embody a symbolic representation of the meaning of love and marriage.*

Breaking a Glass
The traditional Jewish wedding ceremony includes a "breaking of the
glass." Here the groom, having been offered a glass on a wooden pallet or
wrapped in a cloth napkin, smashes it with his foot. The breaking of the
glass symbolizes the fragility of life, the fact that whatever we see before us
as whole can be rendered broken at any moment. It calls our attention to
the need for care toward one another; for just as a glass can be shattered
with a single blow, so the grace of the marriage bond can be destroyed with
a single infidelity or repeated large or small acts of emotional irresponsibil-
ity.

The Chinese Wedding Goblet
In the traditional Chinese ceremony, the bride and groom are presented
with two goblets of honey and wine that are tied together with a red ribbon. At some point in the ceremony, they drink together from the goblets.
In the Chinese symbology of color, red is the color of courage and joy.
Thus, the sharing of the wedding cup means that in marriage the bride and
groom are coming together not only in the joy of love, but also in the
courage it will inevitably require.

The Flower-Strewn Path
In the past in England, a bride and her bridesmaids would walk to the
church on a path strewn with flowers. What is symbolized here is the wish
that the bride's path through life be like a "bed of roses"—a life of ease and
grace. Also, the extravagance of "wasting" the flowers by walking on them

symbolizes the wish that life may be so full and easy that the bride and groom may pass through it as if tiptoeing on flowers.

A Wedding Cup

In an old French custom, the bride and groom drink a toast from a two-handled cup. This, of course, stands for the coming together of their two lives, as a cup is often the symbol of the cup of life. In the French tradition this special cup is called the couple de marriage; it is often handed down as an heirloom to the next generation of brides and grooms.

Wedding Candles

In both Greece and Germany, the bride and groom traditionally greet one another with candles festooned with ribbons and flowers. These symbolize not only the love and delight with which the man and woman are coming together in marriage, but also the illumination they will bring to one another.

The Thrones of Blessing

In the Netherlands both bride and groom sit on grand chairs, or thrones, under a canopy of green boughs. There, together, they receive the well-wishes of family and friends. This custom, symbolizing the evergreen freshness and vitality of love, is usually the high point of a pre-wedding gathering. It sends the bride and groom off to their wedding awash in good wishes, blessed and encouraged in their undertaking.

The Two-Bouquet Ceremony

In Burma both the bride and the groom hold flower bouquets during the recitation of their vows. The symbolism here is that the blessings and obligations of marriage apply to both bride and groom; the promises they make to each other are as precious to the man as they are to the woman. When they have finished their vows, the bride and groom dip their hands in a shared bowl of water, to symbolize the water of life.

A Canopy of Love

In the Jewish wedding, the ceremony takes place under a beautiful silk or velvet canopy, or *huppah*. This represents the home that the bride and groom are creating, and, during the ceremony itself, provides the sacred environment in which the bride and groom exchange their rings and take their vows.

Confetti of Flowers

In India, where the fragrance of flowers in the form of incense is deeply a part of spiritual life, the groom's brother traditionally sprinkles flower petals on the bride and groom at the closing of the wedding ceremony. This is as if to say, through the extravagance of spilled flowers: May your life together be filled with comfort and ease; may it be filled with the deliciousness of flowers; may you want for nothing.

Hindu weddings in India and elsewhere also include an initial exchange of flower garlands by bride and groom, a gift of protective amulets tied to the wrists of the couple, and a recitation of family lineage. The couple is then tied together with a sash, and they walk around a ceremonial fire seven times to signify their vow to face life's challenges together.

Daphne Rose Kingma is the author of *Weddings from the Heart*.

⌒∞⌒

Our wedding day was one of the most beautiful days in the autumn of 1932. The temperature was mild and the sun was not too hot. We were preparing for the wedding the entire week before. Every night in the evening women gathered in my father's house to sing and dance, and the men gathered in his older brother's house to do the same.

Two days before the wedding the Sheikh (a person in charge of conducting ceremonies) came to

"We would not have changed anything."

my father's house with my husband-to-be, his brother-in-law, my uncle, and his older brother. They asked me if I was willingly and freely getting married to the individual in front of me without any pres-

The 1932 wedding license, with loving fingerprints.

sure. I replied in a soft voice, "Yes." The marriage contract was ready and we all signed.

Two days later we got married. We had a typical Muslim and Arabic wedding. I wore a white dress with a white head cover and a black robe over it. I wore the black robe out of my father's house, and when I entered my husband-to-be's home, I removed the coat, which is an older Arabic tradition. It was everything I expected. I would not have changed anything.

—Mahliha Almasri
Amman, Jordan

At the wedding banquet, everyone kept toasting us, saying "Gorka! Gorka!" which is a signal for the bride and groom to kiss. As long as the guests are still chanting Gorka! you have to keep kissing. It means "bitter," so you have to kiss sweet. The whole wedding people kept saying "Gorka!" A hundred times at least. The only time I remember seeing Sergei that night was when we kissed.

—Ekaterina Gordeeva, married to Sergei
Grinkov from 1991 until his death
in 1995

∽✎∾

Wedding Rings in the Woods
BY DAVID MORRIS

My wife and I were married by a country preacher named Jack. No, I'm not kidding. In fact, Jack wasn't even licensed to perform weddings at the time. A pastor friend of his observed as the "official officiant" and signed our marriage certificate. But Jack Glover was a friend, someone we could trust, someone who had a deep and lively passion for God. There was a freshness, humor, and enthusiasm with which he delivered his words at our wedding—all twenty minutes worth. Jack was perfect.

Our outdoor service was delayed twenty minutes while a brief cloudburst doused our wooded park with water and left a fine mist rising up from the ground. With the soothing sounds of a newly replenished river in the background, a flutist began the ceremony with a lilting, meditative piece by Bach. Her father at her side, Lisa came down the aisle between the rows of plastic folding chairs and met me up front. Lisa's mother stood at her side, my father at mine.

The music stopped and a captivating quiet filled our ears. With a paperback Bible and a small set of notes on pink paper as his only props, Jack began his sermon. Alacrity and verve propelled him through a message about the importance of service: to each other as husband and wife, to others, and to God. Jack drew his illustrations from everyday life; they demonstrated the utter simplicity and selflessness with which we should care for others. When he finished speaking, Lisa and I looked each other in the eye and read our straight-from-the-heart vows of love and commitment. We exchanged rings, and were pronounced husband and wife.

"Southern fried chicken, a bluegrass band, and the priceless gift of love."

To symbolize the theme of service, we washed each other's feet in cold water brought up from the river, just as Jesus did to the disciples. A foot washing was a special practice my father encouraged in the Grace Brethren church where he had served as pastor.

This was a wedding with little pretension. The beauty and peace of the setting, the earnestness of Jack, and the joy of the blessed event disarmed us all. Weddings are often such carefully orchestrated affairs. They are high church, even solemn, with a compelling holiness in all that attention to detail and liturgy. In our ceremony, by contrast, I found that holiness, palpable and real, could also come from things commonplace and informal. I like to think that the effervescence of our wedding came out of and amplified a love just as down-to-earth, one that has seen Lisa and I through twelve years of marriage and hopefully many more. That kind of simple love is a priceless, godly gift to be protected and cared for. It's what I like most about being married.

My only very common regret about our wedding is that I didn't relax and enjoy it more. You would have thought it should have been easy. Our reception included Southern fried chicken, shredded pork BBQ, baked beans, coleslaw, and a bluegrass band. We even brought a half-keg of beer, which never ran dry as if Jesus himself kept refilling it. What were we thinking?

David Morris, an editor at Guideposts Books and Inspirational Media Division in New York City, has been married to Lisa since 1988.

⬥

Our wedding was a precious moment filled with feelings of completeness.

> —Rachel Robinson, married to Jackie from
> 1946 until his death in 1972

In Gaither Chapel at eight-thirty in the evening, amid candles and clematis, my beloved Florida mentor, Dr. John Minder, pronounced us husband and wife. . . . It was the most memorable day of my life.

> —Billy Graham, married to Ruth Bell
> Graham since 1943

I should look more often at my wedding pictures. Like most people, I get them out only to show others who ask to see them. But every time I turn the thick pages of that album and see our happy faces, the smiles of those who love us witnessing our vows, I am reconnected to the hope and passion that fuel marriage. It is all there in our faces—it's why so many people ask to see wedding photographs. It is always a comfort and an inspiration to recall that day of promises made, surrounded by those who raised us to the point where we could make them.

—Toni Sciarra Poynter

It was so lovely walking down the steps with Daddy into that group. I wouldn't change the dress, the veil, the flowers (that Elisabeth did so beautifully—columbine and larkspur), or any of it. Cutting the cake, kissing everyone! . . . It was all perfect.

—Anne Morrow Lindbergh,
married to Charles Lindbergh
from 1929 until his death in 1974

Just before the wedding was over, my daughter went to the microphone. She spoke softly, "Instead of throwing the bridal bouquet, I want to give it to my mother and thank her for always being there for me."

There were tears in her eyes. And in mine.

Nothing is easy. Not even happiness.

—Ilene Beckerman

May you be poor in misfortune
Rich in blessings
Slow to argue
and quick to forgive.
But rich or poor
quick or slow
May you know nothing but happiness
from this day forward.

—Irish blessing

Celebrity to One

BY RABBI SHMULEY BOTEACH

The essence of a relationship is to be a celebrity—a celebrity only to one person. There's this man to whom you're famous. He puts your picture up on his wall, saves your silly mementos, stares at you when you're both out in public. When you walk into the room he drops everything to notice you. And he's totally absorbed by your presence.

A celebrity to one might have only one fan, but that fan is a *real* fan—one who's never going to drop you for a younger starlet. If you go bankrupt or develop three chins, your devoted fan will stick around. If you suffer public ridicule, she won't abandon you. As you grow older, your picture won't come down from the wall and be replaced by a picture of a newer quarterback. . . .

Unhealthy fame leads to reclusiveness. But healthy fame leads to the opposite. When you find that one big fan that you've always been looking for—when you enter into a relationship in which someone admires and cherishes you—instead of hiding, you learn to open up. Rather than become cynical, you learn to trust. This intimate and devoted fan that you've been fortunate to acquire doesn't want to take anything from you, only to give. Your happiness becomes that person's happiness.

Being a celebrity to one probably won't get you your own television show. Nor will it get the maitre d' to save you that exclusive table near the fireplace or make strangers come up to you on the street asking for your autograph. But no matter what you do and where you go, you'll always have a fan club right there in the privacy and comfort of your own home.

Chapter Six

LOVE STYLES OF THE RICH AND FAMOUS—AND WE'RE ALL RICH AND FAMOUS

My whole heart rises up in thankfulness.

Robert Browning

He is really generous. He really loves me home with him, but he can get so excited about my work, which means a lot to me. He'll go on about what *I'm* doing, "This is great, this is great!" I play in a very different arena than he does. Our sandboxes are different, but the sands get mixed up and it's fun.

—Kate Capshaw, married to Steven
Spielberg since 1991

We not only love each other, we really like and respect each other. My husband has a delicious sense of humor, and he appreciates mine. I think he's the best company in the world, and he thinks I am.

—Abigail Van Buren ("Dear Abby")

She's the energetic spirit that's contagious; he's the quiet constant. She's the social planner. He's the rational voice. It's like being married to your best friend, your number one supporter, (and your best critic). What a great way to spend 35 years—traveling life's journey together and sharing the same values.

—Tom and Terry Holton
Dayton, Ohio

I loved his sense of humor. He didn't have any false braggadocio.

—Nancy O'Connor, married to Carroll
O'Connor from 1951 until his death
in 2001

It is great to have a helpmate. If either of us has a problem, the other one can help. And Jane is a great cook, which has helped sustained our 56 years together.

—Sylvan Connair
Miamisburg, Ohio

We made a bargain for life. I got the better part of the deal.

—Christopher Reeve, married to Dana
since 1992

Being married means I can break wind and eat ice cream in bed.

—Brad Pitt, married to Jennifer Aniston
since 2000

⟨∞⟩

Ten Great Marriages of the Twentieth Century

BY THERESE J. BORCHARD

An aspiring golfer spends many days watching Jack Nicklaus videos and the PGA Tour to learn how to improve his game. A serious pianist commits many hours studying the masterpieces of Chopin, Mozart, and Beethoven. And an artist spends many afternoons at an art exhibit gazing at the works of Monet, Picasso, or Rembrandt.

The best way to learn a craft is by watching the experts. Here, then, are ten famous couples who have mastered the art of marriage, and can teach all of us a little something about the trade.

In compiling the list, I didn't look for perfect marriages. These ten marriages contain a mix of all the contemporary complications that challenge couples today, from stressful careers to illnesses to kids from previous marriages. But these marriages are great because of the couples' perseverance through thick and thin, sickness and health, bad days and good days, and never losing sight of the commitment they made the day they said, "I do." And, marvelously, the love they have shared spreads out to others, in art or inspiration or great works of compassion.

© TIMEPIX (HULTON/ARCHIVE)

Linda Eastman and Paul McCartney (March 12, 1969). In their twenty-nine years of marriage, Linda and Paul McCartney spent only eleven days apart. Absolutely incredible when you consider all of the hours Paul spent on the road as a member of the hottest band of his time and in his post-Beatle life as a successful musician. For him, Linda's companionship meant everything and was the inspiration behind his music. The songwriter once said in an interview, "Any love song I write is written for Linda."

But everything wasn't always as rosy as it sounded in Paul's lyrics. The public objected to Paul's marrying Linda, especially as he was the last unattached Beatle. They much preferred his former girlfriend Jane Asher to this blond divorcee. And raising four kids in the public spotlight wasn't easy. Paul once said, "You get this picture of us swanning along in a little rowboat managing to avoid the white water, but we were right in the middle of the white water, so it's even more miraculous that we made it." However, in their almost three decades together, the two were known as rock music's most successful couple, until the very end when Linda died of breast cancer in 1998.

Coretta Scott and Martin Luther King, Jr. (June 18, 1953).

On the way back from their first date, Martin Luther King said quietly but confidently to Coretta Scott, "You have everything I have ever wanted in a wife." He had four items on his checklist—character, intelligence, personality, and beauty—and she had them all. From an early age he knew who he was and what kind of woman would make him happy. But Coretta wasn't so sure. Music was her passion, and training her voice her

FROM THE CORETTA SCOTT KING COLLECTION. LICENSE GRANTED BY INTELLECTUAL PROPERTIES MANAGEMENT, ATLANTA, GEORGIA, AS EXCLUSIVE LICENSOR OF THE KING ESTATE.

top priority as a performing arts major at the New England Conservatory of Music. However, it didn't take her long to fall in love with the man who would later spearhead the civil rights movement, and from that point on she never wanted to be anything but "the wife of Martin Luther King," no matter what danger and difficulty lie ahead.

It was Coretta's uncompromising support and encouragement of a greater good that solidified their marriage, even as their home was attacked, their children threatened, and Martin was jailed. King writes in his autobiography, "I am convinced that if I had not had a wife with the fortitude, strength, and calmness of Corrie, I could not have withstood the ordeals and tensions surrounding the movement. . . . If I have done anything in this struggle, it is because I have had behind me and at my side a devoted, understanding, dedicated, patient companion in the person of my wife." Even beyond Martin's death in 1968, Coretta continued to march and speak on behalf of civil and human rights, keeping his dream alive; she also built the Atlanta-based King Center for Non-Violent Social Change, and led the effort to establish the Martin Luther King national holiday.

Rosalynn Smith and Jimmy Carter (July 7, 1946). She fell in love with his picture long before she laid eyes on him in person. Three years his junior, she was best friends with his younger sister, Ruth, who encouraged a romance between the two, until Rosalynn and Jimmy fell madly in love for real and planned to get married. All of the Carters weren't thrilled, as they had big plans for Jimmy, and marrying an eighteen-year-old

girl from Plains, Georgia, was not part of them. But the head- and heart-strong couple walked down the aisle anyway and began their married life in Norfolk, Virginia, where Jimmy was an instructor in naval programs.

Two decades and four kids later, Jimmy

entered politics. He became governor of Georgia in 1971, and the thirty-ninth president of the United States in 1977. Throughout the presidency, Rosalynn was not just First Lady, but his main advisor, translating the hopes and dreams of the American people to the leader of the nation. As best friends and soul mates, they remain one of the country's strongest teams today, involved in volunteer services, from building low-income housing to continuing mediation for human rights and peace in the Middle East.

Joanne Woodward and Paul Newman (January 29, 1958). Joanne and Paul. Paul and Joanne. Their names belong together, as they have become one of America's most adored couples. And so you would expect their beginning to be a "love at first sight" tale, not the "I hated him on sight" story Joanne tells. The two were briefly introduced to each other by Maynard Morris, a well-known talent agent, and then cast together in the Broadway production *Picnic*. Since Paul had been married for three years and was the father of three children, the two simply became good friends.

However when Paul and his wife separated, the friendship intensified and blossomed into a full-fledged love affair that would soon unite them in the minds and hearts of fans throughout the country. By the time they finished working on the movie *The Long Hot Summer*, the couple decided to marry. And since that happy civil ceremony in Las Vegas, the couple has loved each other for three decades, made many movies together, raised three children, and contributed their time, talent, and money to numerous charities.

Rachel Isum and Jackie Robinson (February 10, 1946). It was more than talent that made Jackie Robinson a baseball legend as the Brooklyn Dodger who heroically broke baseball's color line. As he saw it, his success was due in large part to the most important woman of his life, Rachel Isum. "I know that every successful man is supposed to say that without his wife he could never have accomplished success," he writes in his autobiography. "It is gospel in my case. . . . She has been strong, loving, gentle, and brave, never afraid to either criticize or comfort me."

Confronted by prejudice throughout his entire career as the first black man to break into the white world of sports, he patiently endured the pain of racism. But he had at least one faithful and supportive fan in the stands throughout his entire life: the nursing student he met in 1940 who would eventually become his beloved wife. When he tired of the insults, he would turn to this partner and best friend, who, he once said, "keeps me sane."

When the couple's eldest child, Jackie Jr., twenty-four, died in a car crash, the famous pitcher and his wife would tackle another kind of tragedy, but emerged from their grief an even stronger pair. Only one year later, Rachel lost her beloved husband, but her dedication to him has continued for three decades in her work for the Jackie Robinson Foundation, which provides educational and leadership opportunities for minority students nationwide.

Gilda Radner and Gene Wilder (September 18, 1984).

They were married only five years, but Gilda and Gene had enough love and laughter to teach all married couples a lesson about having fun together and how to keep the party going past the memorial service and a memory alive beyond the funeral.

Gilda Radner had been a fan of Gene Wilder's for many years, but the first time she saw him in person she said, "My heart fluttered—I was hooked. It felt like my life went from black and white to Technicolor." She was "bitten with love" as they made the movie *Hanky Panky* in August 1981, and the brash girl from *Saturday Night Live* turned into "this shy, demure ingénue with knocking knees," she writes in her autobiography. Three years later the couple married in the south of France. The late-night comedienne wanted desperately to start a family with the love of her life, but after two miscarriages and a host of health problems, she was diagnosed with ovarian cancer.

No one was more attentive during her illness than her devoted husband, who stayed beside her every step of her two-year therapy. As her best friend and support system, he knew how to keep her smiling and laughing, even in her worst hours before her death in 1989.

Nancy Davis and Ronald Reagan (March 4, 1952). When

twenty-nine-year-old Nancy Davis found her name listed on the membership rosters of several Communist front groups, she phoned one of her directors, Mervyn LeRoy, who forwarded the problem to the president of the Screen Actors Guild, Ronald Reagan. So Ron took Nancy to dinner and explained the complication, that there were several actresses by the name

Nancy Davis. But the two enjoyed each other's company so
much that the date lasted until
three in the morning. A few
dates later, Ron spontaneously
proposed to Nancy over dinner,
and she accepted.

Friends of this moonstruck
couple figured the gazes and love
notes and flowers would subside
after their honeymoon, but their
affection only intensified—so
public that many reporters believed their love to be at least
partly an act. "But it wasn't—
and it isn't," Nancy writes in her autobiography. How could it be with a
man who admits to missing his wife "if she just steps out of the room," and
leaves numerous notes on her desk signed ITWWW, as in "I love you more
than anything *in the whole wide world.*"

Faced with their most difficult challenge, Ron's Alzheimer's disease, the
couple remained completely committed to each other, and Nancy practiced
something she's always believed: that marriage isn't a fifty-fifty proposition,
because "there are many times when you have to give 90 percent, or when
both of you have to give 90 percent." With a marriage that endured both
Hollywood and the White House, the Reagans contribute one of history's
most beautiful and endearing love stories.

Dale Evans and Roy Rogers (December 31, 1947). She didn't
know how to ride a horse when she became his leading lady, but they were
a hit from the start. The audience loved them as a pair. Their partnership
offstage consisted of a solid friendship at first, since Roy was married with
two small children, and Dale was a single mother of a teenage son.
However, when Roy's wife died after the birth of their third child, the
wholesome on-screen romance became a real-life marriage.

In the fall of 1947, they were on their horses in the chutes at the
Chicago rodeo waiting to be introduced, when Roy confessed his love to
Dale and asked, "What are you doing New Year's Eve?" the title of a popu-

lar love song at the time. In the brief interval between the drum roll and the beginning of the show, she looked at him and said yes to his romantic proposal.

America's King of the Cowboys and the Queen of the West starred in twenty-six movies and three television series. But the happy endings they portrayed on screen didn't always translate into real life. One child was born with Down's syndrome and died a few days before her second birthday; one of the four children they adopted was killed in a bus crash; and another boy they fostered died in the army. But despite their tragedies they continued along their "happy trails" with their children, grandchildren, and great-grandchildren for half a century, contributing much of their time and money to humanitarian efforts, until Roy's death in 1998 and her death three years later.

Ruby Dee and Ossie Davis (December 9, 1948). Not only do their theatrical, screen, and television credits span fifty years, so does their marriage, which, according to Ruby, has "weathered temptation and anger and jealousy, resentment, self-righteousness and a little bit of selfishness." But they've made it this far, and are going strong, as they teach by way of example what it means to be dedicated and committed.

The couple met during the winter of 1945 in New York when both were cast in the New Amsterdam Theater production of *Jeb*. Three years later they were in rehearsal for another play, *The Smile of the World,* and had Thursday off. So they drove to New Jersey and got married. Then back to work the

next day. And, eventually—throughout the next half century—on to collaborate on more than thirty projects for stage, screen, television, and radio, along with raising three children and seven grandchildren.

But they aren't just actors. They are activists. "For us, art was always political," Davis says. "In the black community, art was the one way we could express our humanity." And so they have used their stardom to advance freedom and equality for African Americans. For them, their success as actors and as a married couple is born out of the Struggle, which ties them not only to each other, but also to everyone who seeks justice.

Gracie Allen and George Burns (January 7, 1926).
Together they were one of the most popular and successful comedy acts in history. George Burns, the straight man, with Gracie Allen, a lovable woman smart enough to act dumb. The best team going, on and off the stage, their showbiz marriage lasted for thirty-eight years. "Gracie was my partner in our act, my best friend, my life and my lover, and the mother of our two children," George writes in *Gracie: A Love Story*. "She made me famous as the only man in America who could get a laugh by complaining, 'My wife understands me.'" But perhaps his sweetest sound bite is his simple answer on how to make a marriage work: "It's easy," he said, "marry Gracie." And taking his own words to heart, he never married again after her death in 1964.

⌐◇¬

> When I first met John, I couldn't believe life could be this much fun. . . . There's always a game to play and something fun to do—a way to look at life with joyous eyes. He wants to make things fun.
> —Kelly Preston, married to John Travolta
> since 1991

He said one time, "It's incredible when somebody walks in a room and all you feel is good about them." All I feel is good. When I was

a little girl, I fantasized what I wanted one day in a husband. I've found that. And I met him when I'd given up on ever finding him.
—Mary Steenburgen, married to
Ted Danson since 1995

I love everything about him. He's a good father, a good husband, a good provider, a good lover, a good friend . . . everything you want, and he has been for 35 years.
—Viola Hernandez
Grand Rapids, Michigan

Marrying Ben was the best thing I ever did. He's my most precious possession. I am the luckiest person in the whole world.
—Betty Moore
Annapolis, Maryland

We're deeply in love. We were when we got married and it stayed that way.
—Tom Brokaw, married to Meredith
for more than 35 years

I fall in love with her every day.
—Tom Hanks, married to
Rita Wilson since 1988

I've been in love before—but never in love like this before.
—Grace Kelly, married to Prince Rainier III of Monaco from 1956 until her death in 1982

© TIMEPIX (THOMAS D. MCAVOY)

⌒∞⌒

Inspired Love Letters

I love you with a love beyond the limits of imagination, that every minute of my life is consecrated to you, that never an hour passes without my thinking of you. . . . That you, you alone, and all of you, as I see you, as you are—only you can please me, absorb the faculties of my soul; that you pervade my soul to its farthest reaches; that there is no corner of my heart into which you do not see, no thought of mine which is not subordinate to you. That my arms, my strength, my mind are all yours. That my soul lives in your body, and that the day upon which you should change or cease to live would be the day of my death. That the world is beautiful only because you inhabit it. . . . A magnetic fluid flows between persons who love each other.

—Napoleon Bonaparte

My darling Clemmie,

A year to-day my lovely white pussy-cat came to me, and I hope and pray she may find on this September morning no cause—however vague or secret—for regrets. The bells of this old city are ringing now and they recall to my mind the chimes which saluted our wedding and the crowds of cheering people. A year has gone—and if it has not brought you all the glowing and perfect joy which fancy paints, still it has brought a clear bright light of happiness and some great things. My precious and beloved Clemmie my earnest desire is to enter still more completely into your dear heart and nature and to curl myself up in your darling arms. I feel so safe with you and I do not keep the slightest disguise. You have been so sweet and good to me that I cannot say how grateful I feel to you for your dear nature, and matchless beauty. Not please disdain the caresses of your devoted pug.

> Always my own darling
> Clem-puss-bird
> Your loving husband
> W [Winston Churchill]

My noble, incomparable Edith,

I do not know how to express or analyze the conflicting emotions that have surged like a storm through my heart all night long. I only know that first and foremost in all my thoughts has been the glorious confirmation you gave me last night—without effort, unconsciously, as of course—of all I have ever thought of your mind and heart.

You have the greatest soul, the noblest nature, the sweetest, most loving heart I have ever known, and my love, my reverence, my admiration for you, you have increased in one evening as I should have thought only a lifetime of intimate, loving association could have increased them.

You are more wonderful and lovely in my eyes than you ever were before; and my pride and joy and gratitude that you should love me with such a perfect love are beyond all expression, except in some great poem which I cannot write.

Your own,
Woodrow [Wilson]

Darling, I miss you so much. In fact, much too much for my own good. I never realized that you were such an intimate part of my life. My life without you is like a year without a spring time which comes to give illumination and heat to the atmosphere saturated by the dark cold breeze of winter. . . . O excuse me, my darling. I didn't mean to go off on such a poetical and romantic flight. But how else can we express the deep emotions of life other than in poetry? Isn't love too ineffable to be grasped by the cold calculating hands of intellect?

—Martin Luther King, Jr.

My darling Bar,
This should be a very easy letter to write—words should come easily and in short it should be simple for me to tell you how desperately happy I was to open the paper and see the announcement of our engagement, but somehow I can't possibly say all in a letter I should like to.

I love you, precious, with all my heart and to know that you love me means my life. How often I have thought about the immeasurable joy that will be ours some day. How lucky our children will be to have a mother like you—

As the days go by the time of our departure draws nearer. For a long time I had anxiously looked forward to the day when we would go aboard and set to sea. It seemed that obtaining that goal would be all I could desire for some time, but, Bar, you have changed all that. I cannot say that I do not want to go—for that would be a lie. . . . I do want to go because it is my part, but now leaving presents itself not as an adventure but as a job which I hope will be over before long. Even now, with a good while between us and the sea, I am thinking of getting back. This may sound melodramatic, but if it does it is only my inadequacy to say what I mean. Bar, you have made my life full of everything I could ever dream of—my complete happiness should be a token of my love for you. . . .

Goodnite, my beautiful. . . . All my love darling—

Poppy, public fiancé as of 12/12/43
[George Bush]

My Darling,

This is really just an "in between" day. It is a day on which I love you three hundred and sixty five days more than I did a year ago and three hundred sixty five less than I will a year from now.

But I wonder how I lived at all for all the three hundred and sixty fives before I met you.

All my love,
Your Husband [Ronald Reagan]

On Marriage

BY KAHLIL GIBRAN

You were born together, and together you shall be forevermore.
You shall be together when the white wings of death scatter your days.
Ay, you shall be together even in the silent memory of God.
But let there be spaces in your togetherness,
And let the winds of the heavens dance between you.
Love one another, but make not a bond of love:
Let it rather be a moving sea between the shores of your souls.
Fill each other's cup but drink not from one cup.
Give one another of your bread but eat not from the same loaf.
Sing and dance together and be joyous, but let each one of you be alone,
Even as the strings of a lute are alone though they quiver with the same
music.
Give your hearts, but not into each other's keeping.
For only the hand of Life can contain your hearts.
And stand together yet not too near together:
For the pillars of the temple stand apart,
And the oak tree and the cypress grow not in each other's shadow.

Chapter Seven

LOVE KNOWS NO OBSTACLES

> The greatest good
> you can do for others
> is not just to share
> your riches
> but to reveal to them
> their own.
> — Disraeli

Married to Laughter
BY JERRY STILLER

When I got back to New York at the end of the summer of 1953, I was in love with someone whose impulses were pure and trusting. I couldn't believe what was happening to me.

87

I started wondering if this was permanent. One night after Anne asked me over for dinner, I remarked casually, "Have you ever been with anyone else?"

"Yes," she said.

I paused. I hadn't really expected she would say no.

"What was he like?" I asked, almost not wanting to hear the answer. "He was an artist. He wore glasses and his eyes ran." It was a joke to make me feel better? To reassure me that their relationship was over?

"What happened?" I asked.

"He left." There was sadness in her voice.

I asked myself if I could be with someone who had been with another man. Was she still in love with him?

"He was the only one," she said, as if guessing my thoughts. "I must tell you something else."

"What?"

"My mother committed suicide."

We silently looked at one another. I took her hand and held it.

"Do you still want to see me?" she said, as if everything we'd had would end.

"Of course," I said. I couldn't comprehend anything that was happening. I could only sit and listen. For a moment I wanted to escape. What was I getting myself into? Until now this had been crazy fun, a crazy adventure. A girl I'd met at an agent's office liked me. Now it was becoming a little too much. She was so free and open about her feelings. I was scared. Should I stop something beautiful, or should I trust? I wanted to leave, but I knew there would be tears if I did. Did I want to see her cry? Could I say, "I never want to see you again"? But I couldn't leave. I didn't know why.

The following weeks we said little but saw each other a lot. I started thinking about my parents, and what my mother, who was ill with cancer, would do if she knew I was seeing a Christian girl. Although Anne had introduced me to her father, I couldn't bring myself to do the same with my mother. So I kept putting it off, thinking nothing was going to come of the relationship.

I tried to stop seeing Anne because of this, but she'd call or I'd call and we'd meet and walk around the Village. It felt so good being near her.

One day we were on a bus that made its last stop at Fifth Avenue and 23rd Street. We had been to a museum uptown. I had literally spent the last dime that I'd made that summer. While still on the bus I looked at the Flatiron Building and thought, *I know how to lose her. I'm busted, no job. When I tell her, she'll leave me. I'll tell her I want to break it off.*

"We're breaking up," I said.

"This you tell me on a bus?"

"Yeah."

"Why?"

I looked at her. Her face was like that of a beautiful spaniel with sad eyes. "I'm broke. I can't support you. There's nothing going for us."

"Why don't you marry me?" was her answer.

"What?! That's crazy."

"Why? I love you and I want you to marry me."

"What if I said I can't?"

"Then we can't go on like this."

I felt something drop inside me. I saw myself without her, and a feeling of emptiness suddenly swept through me.

"How could we live?" I asked.

"Don't worry about it," she said. "My father will help us. We'll live in my apartment. I own the lease."

What was happening? She had just proposed to me. I was penniless, but she loved me. It was a moment I never dreamed would happen.

"We can do it right away," Anne said. "We can go to City Hall. We'll get married. I want to meet your mother."

I wasn't sure how meeting Anne and the news of our upcoming marriage would affect my mother.

"She's got cancer and she's going to die, Anne." It was the first time I had allowed myself to talk about my mother.

Then my fear of really losing Anne frightened me.

"Okay," I said, "you'll meet her."

At the apartment in the Ravenswood Project in Queens, my mother was sitting at the kitchen table by the window. She didn't look well. My father had not yet come home from work.

"Mom, I'd like you to meet Anne."

"Forgive me," my mother said in perfect English. "I can't get up."

"I understand," Anne said.

"Please, won't you sit down?" There was a formality in my mother's voice that I had never noted before. I could tell she knew why we were here.

"You love my son?" she said. The question was so immediate and direct that it pierced my sensibilities.

"I want to marry Jerry," Anne said.

There were no answering words, no cry of protest. I could see tears in my mother's brown eyes. They steadfastly refused to fall; my mother's eyes seemed magnified.

"You love each other?" she finally said.

"Yes. I'll make Jerry a good wife."

My mother looked at me. I could not tell what was going through her mind.

"Do you like matzohs?" she said after a while, breaking off a piece and handing it to Anne. "We keep them around even if it's not Passover."

Anne broke a little piece off that piece and ate it.

"Two people must really love each other," my mother said after another long interval. "That's all that counts."

"Will you come to the wedding?" Anne asked.

"We'll be there."

Anne and my mother kissed.

Three weeks later, on September 14, 1953, we were married. The wedding took place at City Hall. The judge's chambers were in an office high up in the Municipal Building. It was a space with file cabinets and wooden desks. There were civil-service employees bustling about. Why this bland setting to consummate the feelings we had for each other? As the ceremony was about to begin, the office emptied. The clerks sensed the need for privacy and disappeared into the hallways.

Willie, Bella, Ed Meara, and Ursula Campbell and her husband, Pat, arrived. Anne had known Ursula ever since arriving in Manhattan at age eighteen from Rockville Centre to study acting with Alfred Linder from the Dramatic Workshop. Willie and Bella were meeting Ed for the first time. There were smiles and polite conversation. They were standing together in a corner of the room. What could they be saying? At least they were speaking. They could have been ignoring one another, destroying us by silence. As I went over to them I overheard my mother saying, "What do you think, Mr. Meara?"

"They're just a couple of crazy kids," Ed said.

Suddenly all three were laughing out loud. I wanted to hug all of them. I could feel the leap they had made to get to this juncture.

"When this is over," Ed said, "we're going over to the Republican Club for a wedding breakfast."

My father, the lifelong Democrat, asked, "Are we going to have bacon?"

Was it a joke to break the ice another inch?

"No, Mr. Stiller," Ed said earnestly. "We don't eat bacon in our house. It can give you trichinosis."

Judge Ben Shalleck, the uncle of Alan Shalleck, a close buddy of mine from Syracuse, was a former husband of Lillian Roth, the legendary saloon singer. He arrived to perform the ceremony. It seemed to stamp the moment with some sort of showbizzy significance.

"Did you pay the clerk?" Judge Shalleck asked.

I told him I hadn't.

"That's okay, it'll be my wedding present to you. What about the blood test? You've got the results?"

"I do," I said. Ten days earlier Anne and I had gone to Bendiner and Schlesinger, the pharmacists near Cooper Square, and the results were fine.

"Good." The judge's voice now took on an official tone. He conducted a simple ceremony, and Anne and I exchanged vows. When it was over we all piled into a car and headed for the

Anne and Jerry, married to laughter since 1953. ©TIMEPIX
(DAVID ALLOCCA)

Republican Club. I looked over at Anne and knew I would never be alone again.

Jerry Stiller, known to the current generation as George Costanza's father on *Seinfeld,* is one half of the legendary comic team Stiller and Meara. Jerry and Anne Meara were married in 1953. Their real son is the actor Ben Stiller.

⌒❀⌐

I was aware that I wasn't liked . . . (Some people) really wished me harm . . . It was rough, but there was always one person in England who was there for me, and it was enough.

—Linda McCartney, married to Paul from
1969 until her death in 1998

People preferred Jane Asher. Jane Asher fitted. She was a better Fergie. Linda wasn't a very good Fergie for me and people generally tended to disapprove of me marrying a divorcee and an American. That wasn't too clever. None of that made a blind bit of difference; I actually just liked her, I still do, and that's all it's to do with.

—Paul McCartney

Our love survived all the talk, but it was pretty violent. I mean it was pretty nasty, a lot of it, and we almost went under. But we managed to survive and here we are, and we're thankful.

—John Lennon, married to Yoko Ono
from 1969 until his death in 1980

When two are gathered together, there is nothing you can't do. As a power it is very strong.

—Yoko Ono

⌒∞⌒

A Public Union

BY MARGOT SCHWAAB SAGE-EL

We were sitting on our front steps, watching the kids play and feeling the warmth of an afternoon sun. It had been one of the harder years: the kids were approaching their teens, and we were both embarking on new careers. It seemed as though we never had time for us, and yet I was overwhelmed with gratitude that we were still together. In twenty years, our marriage had gone through many stages and transcended many obstacles. But Barry and I made a commitment to each other, and when our children arrived, we made a commitment to them. We have always tried to honor that.

One of the interesting aspects of our marriage is that we are in a public union as well as a private one. We are an interracial couple. I am Caucasian, of German descent, and Barry is African American, from Southern and Caribbean Island families. We met as students at Columbia University in 1975, in Spanish class. Opposites attract: he was suave, urbane, and guarded; I was naive, eager, and candid. We fell in love immediately.

While our dating and marriage were private decisions, the fact that we were interracial invited scrutiny, speculation, and expectations from others but not necessarily in a negative way. We have had challenges but surprisingly few objections, at least not openly antagonistic ones. Initially our parents were not happy and we kept our relationship to ourselves while we were in school and still learning about each other. By the time we married in 1981 everyone was happy for us. We were surrounded by two loving families and a safety net of good friends.

In our private moments, we rejoiced and struggled in our togetherness. We were young when we met and committed to each other immediately. The early years offered all the excitement of being in love, with the full bloom of passion. We were living in New York, starting our lives as adults, establishing our careers, meeting friends, going out dancing, walking through Central Park, visiting museums. Like any married couple, we were also working out our expectations of each other, emotionally and practically. Did a fight mean a breakup, should we have joint or separate banking accounts, who should clean the bathroom, prepare the meals, which holidays should we spend with which family?

In a few years we moved to Brooklyn and started our family. Trevor was born in 1985 and Maddie in 1987. Those years were full of physically hard work, but emotionally they were gentle and loving and filled with hope. They were also the years we came to realize what a public statement it was having biracial children. While our families embraced our children unwaveringly, their existence catapulted us into a political statement with the rest of society. Our children had the burden of being seen as the hope of the future; the translators between races, the commercially touted Colors of the World.

As our children reached school age, we moved to suburban Montclair, New Jersey, a racially mixed suburb known for its welcoming atmosphere. Our daughter Olivia was born in 1992 and our lives settled down to the steady rhythm of schools, activities, church, family, and work. Our marriage truly became a working partnership. These were less glamorous times, with fewer intimate moments and more nuts-and-bolts tasks. We celebrated accomplishments, nursed setbacks, and worked to keep going. During this time we have been drawn into the most public period of our lives. As our children entered the school system, as their status as neither black nor white required concrete identification, and as we became aware of the inequities of the races in our society, we realized we had to become our own advocates and work actively within our society to right what we perceived wrong.

Our neighborhood in Brooklyn had been predominantly black. But in Montclair we lived in a predominantly white neighborhood and in this racially mixed town, which had worked very hard since the 1970s to achieve successful integration in the schools, race was still a thorny issue. We were shocked to become aware of the inequities, or benign but powerful differences, between the treatments of the races in the suburbs. While the schools struggled to close the achievement gap, some teachers still ostracized the energetic black boys as troubled underachievers. When I was not with my family, and therefore white, I experienced privileges that I hadn't been aware existed. When I was with my family, thus rendered non-white, we were treated differently. After sorting out our new experiences, Barry and I realized that we couldn't just accept the status quo. We were fortunate to join a group of committed and dedicated people through our Unitarian church to found the Undoing Racism Committee. Through workshops, outreach, and study we have been able to

"To us, it just made our marriage work."

start to effect some change in the community. Personally, the involvement has strengthened our children and us. Our informed awareness has helped us sort out situations and work towards solutions, whether they are innocent comments or overt actions. Our children recognize and confront racist actions, they are confident to identify as biracial with both African-American and Caucasian friends, and they have learned to speak up for themselves.

Of course, these activities highlighted our public union, making us the interracial poster-family, an example that integration can work, etc. However, to us, it just made our marriage work. We realize that as a part of our union, we do have larger responsibilities. We each still have visions of a utopian society, a society where one's race is a celebrated part of one's identity and not a marker of socioeconomic-political boundaries. Through our union, we have made a commitment to work towards this goal.

I like being married because I like being in a partnership. I like building a life together: blending families and traditions, raising children, creating a homestead, and developing a history together. I like sharing ideas with someone I respect, and having someone I love challenge and support me. We have memories of a quarter of a century together, and, more than ever, have great hope for the future.

Margot Schwaab Sage-El, married to Barry since 1981, is founder and owner of Watchung Booksellers, a community independent bookstore in Montclair, New Jersey.

❦

You all know the reasons which have impelled me to renounce the Throne. But I want you to understand that in making up my mind, I did not forget the country or the Empire which as Prince of Wales, and lately as King, I have for twenty-five years tried to serve. But you must believe me when I tell you that I have found it impossible to carry the heavy burden of responsibility and to discharge my duties as King as I would wish to do without the help and support of the woman I love [Wallis Simpson].

—King Edward VIII (abdication speech)

Darling—

My heart is so full of love for you and the agony of not being able to see you after all you have been through is pathetic. At the moment we have the whole world against us and our love. . . . We will find something for you, my darling, and I am feeling all your feelings of loneliness and despair which must face you on this new beginning. If we could have been together during the waiting it would have been so much easier. I long for you so. I hear that there is an organization of women who have sworn to kill me. Evans is investigating. We must not take any risks because to have an accident come now would be too much to bear. . . . Your broadcast was very good, my angel, and it is all going to be so very lovely. I hope you will never regret this sacrifice. . . . It is worth it, God knows, with all these threatening letters. I love you David and am holding so tight.

—Wallis [Simpson]

❦

I Married a Hindu
BY JO MCGOWAN

When my husband, Ravi, and I married thirteen years ago, we had plenty of God-given disparities to keep us busy. I was twenty-one and he was thirty-three. I am American and he is from India. I am a Roman Catholic who attends Mass, keeps the prescribed fasts, and uses a breviary. He is a Hindu who prays daily, and abjures temples and idol-worship. I am a college dropout and a professional writer; he is a Ph.D. in metallurgy turned environmentalist activist. We live in India, in the foothills of the Himalayas, on a combined yearly income of somewhat less than $5,000. You would think that when we disagreed, it would be over something substantial—at any rate, something more substantial than a sofa set.

You would be wrong. The sofa set in question belonged to friends, a British couple who had lived in our town for eight years. They had it built their first year here and it had been heavily used by them and their two young boys, a cat, two dogs, and an endless parade of friends. It was, to be sure, an exceptionally comfortable set, deep and roomy, with just the right amounts of sink and spring to encourage leisurely reading, and conversation; but a living room containing it would not be a candidate for a House Beautiful award. I had, though I try not to be materialistic, coveted it since the day they announced that they were being transferred to Africa and intended to sell most of their furniture.

Without exactly discussing it with my husband, I arranged with my friends to buy it for about half what they had paid and perhaps a tenth what it would cost to buy new. When I told Ravi, he said it was up to me, but in his innocence, he assumed I was buying only the couch.

He was at work when it all arrived—an enormous couch and two large chairs which had doubled in size on the trip from my friend's large living room to our small one—and I did my best to make it fit in unobtrusively. But even I had to admit that the effect was a bit staggering. We'll get used to it, I assured him when he walked in and nearly tripped over the chair that was a bit too close to the door for comfort.

Our children, at least, were delighted. They tumbled the length of the couch and did headstands on the chairs, just as I had done in my childhood. And just as my mother had, I scolded them about ruining the springs and pointed out the heel marks on the walls. I gave up rather sooner than she had, however, as it suddenly occurred to me that my concern for furniture was proof of my husband's contention that we were becoming a bourgeois, middle-class family, anxious to acquire symbols of status, eager for a life of indolence and wealth.

Before moving to India, it had never occurred to me that a secondhand, eight-year-old sofa set could be a status symbol. But then again, I grew up in America, where reality is very different. To me, a refrigerator is an absolute necessity; to Ravi, pure luxury.

Over the years (we've lived in India for twelve), we've done our share of compromising. I got the fridge on day one—even a purist like my husband had to concede that expecting a New Englander who wilted in Massachusetts summers to survive in temperatures of 115°F without one was too much—but it was the smallest model. It was I who banned a television, although Ravi would love one (he says he needs it for "information"), and we both agreed not to invest in a car (although I have been less enthusiastic with each additional child; dragging all three on Indian public transport isn't easy).

The discussions we had over each of these items, however, were reasoned and logical and had to do with practical concerns: milk spoiling, the effect of TV on family life, and the convenience of a car vs. the expense and the pollution. We seldom got emotional and we usually could explain ourselves. What we were really talking about was the paradox at the heart of every marriage: the wedding of two entirely different worlds and constant adjustments and fine tuning required to make it all work. In a marriage like ours, however, the requirements are at times, excessive. Worlds farther apart than a Hindu's India and a Catholic's America are hard to imagine, and there are times when I wonder how we ever thought our love could bridge the gap between the two. In our family lore, our favorite stories are of the times we transgressed some deeply held belief of the other's, all the while totally unconscious of having offended.

To his credit, Ravi has proved remarkably open to my preconceived ideas and has more or less gracefully accepted the fact that much is required from both of us. He has occasional relapses when we are with his family; old habits die hard. But I am no longer twenty-one, I speak the language now, and I have made my own adjustments, not the least of which has been learning to make chapattis.

The difficulties of a cross-cultural marriage are enormous, there can be no denying. But the rewards are equally great. When I consider Ravi's virtues as a husband, words like fidelity and devotion come to mind, old-fashioned virtues met less and less frequently in the standard American marriage. Marrying into a traditional culture where marriage is still a sacred bond and divorce still a scandal provides a security that I, for one, am grateful for. The institution is stronger than the individual couple and provides a firm and certain footing which makes it possible to take a great deal for granted.

"Words like fidelity and devotion come to mind."

In America, on the other hand, many couples seem to begin married life with the sense of charting unknown waters, ever mindful of the dangers of the journey and the flimsiness of their vessel. Here in India, the path is so well-worn and safe arrival so virtually assured that one hardly considers the bullock cart one is traveling in. The jolts and occasional breakdowns are expected and taken in stride and there are plenty of fellow pilgrims to ask for directions. And at the end of the day there's that couch to sink into and relax on. Like our marriage, it looks like it's here to stay.

Jo McGowan and her family live in Dehra Dun, India.

 ∞

Kim Hoa and I joined common paths on January 16, 1971, in the Sacred Heart cathedral in her hometown Can Tho, Vietnam. Our countries were at war at the time. She was a social worker; I was a journalist. We met and fell in love.

The marriage of an Asian and an American was less common then. I never thought of it as unusual. Love does that.

My bride was the daughter of an elementary school principal and his loving wife who kept the home running. In 1973 we returned from Vietnam to Detroit, Michigan, where Kim Hoa gave birth to our three children, Daniel, Christine, and Catherine. Each has been an endless treasure, full of life and surprise. They've gone off to school now and we miss them. Now we feed the birds in our back yard. The nurturing instinct does not seem to go away.

Raising children takes energy and patience. The paths they take are not always the ones we might have planned. Being a parent means being there for them, no matter what. That's the lesson we've wanted to teach. Love is forever.

Looking back, I see the world getting smaller as the days go by faster. Life passes in an instant, but God's love, too, endures. So the lessons a parent might pass are simple. If you fall down you get up. If you are on top of the world, enjoy, but don't expect it to last. Love yourself, for you are truly loved.

No doubt there will be more so-called interracial marriages as the world continues to shrink—until one day we wake up to realize there is but one race, the human race, and that race simply does not matter. Each and every one of us is loved.

—Tom Fox
Kansas City, Missouri

I couldn't be married to anyone but Warren nor do I think he could be married to anyone but me. During our twenty-year window on eternity, so far, we have become experts at parties and vacations; we always make their honor roll. We get B's on questions of laundry, housekeeping, whether or not to use a map to get somewhere. And we flunk togetherness on issues of the ultimate: Warren is a devout Jew. I am an ordained minister in the United Church of Christ.

Our differences are many. We love them. He cooks; I don't. Warren does feast; I do leftovers. Warren leaves lights on; I turn them off with a moral vigor that makes Wagnerian operas appear gentle. Still, we need each other. We do not so much complete each other as confuse each other. Since we both love paradox and diversity, we are an ideal couple.

Our children, whom we do not grade, will summarize their parents as follows: "Ask any question. She always says yes, he always says no." In fact, the children have a pretty good stand-up act: the comedy is to introduce any question and then simultaneously say the yes and the no. We didn't want to simply confuse them about their religious origin, me being Christian and he being Jewish and all. We wanted to confuse them deeply.

The chance that our children could ever worship the God with whom we grew up is practically nil. That God is too small. Their world is too large; its size is at their front door or available with a stroke of a key. I did not meet a Moslem until I was thirty: until just recently, my children lived next door to five of them.

We are an interfaith family; so are they. One couple is Jewish and Moslem; the other is Catholic and Moslem. All four, like my children's parents, are firm followers of the God beyond God. We also borrow each other's lawnmowers.

When I think of our marriage, I think of it as gift upon gift upon gift. Not just vacations and not just great dinner parties, not even the joy we have known with and through our children. But gift shaking hands with gift becoming knotted into gift.

Warren and I only get a B on our housekeeping. We are powerfully uncertain about who owns God. Where we excel is at making a home together, for each other, and for a few others as well.

—Donna Schaper
Coral Gables, Florida

René and I knew other very successful couples, such as Eddy and Mia, with an age difference of fifteen, twenty, even thirty years. And there was the example of Charlie Chaplin and Oona O'Neill, who stayed happy together for more than thirty years. They'd even produced a strong, close-knit family.

René told me that when he realized he was falling in love with me, he'd tried to forget me. He'd left for Las Vegas at every opportunity. He'd even gone to Paris and seen Eddy Marnay, whom he'd always thought of as a father and a person in whom he could confide.

"You know Eddy. He and I walked for miles through Paris while I spoke to him about you."

"What did he tell you?"

"He said to me: 'Do you really love her?' "

"And what did you say?"

"I told him: 'I'm crazy about her. I see her everywhere, I think about her all the time.' "

"And he said?"

"He told me: 'If you love her, you've got nothing to fear. You can't hurt her.' "

"That's just what I told you."

But René was also thinking of my career. He thought about it even more than he thought of our happiness, an idea that really crushed me at moments. He thought that if people found out that we were in love, all we'd built would be destroyed.

So for a long time we loved each other only in privacy and in the intimacy of our families. They adjusted to it pretty well, I think. But not me. I suffered and wept, perhaps because I was the younger one. And also because it was my first love. I wanted to shout it from the rooftops on the very first day. To be loved by René Angélil was more beautiful than anything I had known my whole life.

—Celine Dion, married to René Angélil
since 1994

You marry the right person.

—Robert Levine, married to
Mary Tyler Moore since 1983

And it doesn't matter how old he or she is.

—Mary Tyler Moore, 18 years older

Some people were offended that I'd fallen in love with an American and not a Canadian. It didn't matter. I was totally, hopelessly in love with her. Still am.

—Wayne Gretzky, married to
Janet Jones since 1988

Pretty much the first thing I did after I got my dream job was make a really stupid mistake. Our campaign hierarchy was announced the same week James [Carville] was named chief strategist [of the opponent's campaign]. Lois Romano of *The Washington Post* called both of us to get the story. I said to James, "You tell her that we're putting our relationship on hold." All I needed was for the first story of my job to be about me and not the candidate.

James said, "That is very stupid. It's like inviting people to follow us around."

"But we *will* be on hold," I argued, "because that's how presidential races work. And that's why you're a big jerk, and that's why it is stupid for you to take this job after telling me you didn't want to. Because we *are* going to have our relationship on hold, and you don't know what this means. You've worked a bunch of state races. So what? You don't know how terrible a presidential race is." It was a big Miss-Know-It-All speech and I was screaming at him.

The people around me were all giving me professional advice. "If anything goes wrong, if anything leaks, you're going to be blamed. It's not fair. It's terrible, that's just how it works."

Their other line of reasoning went, "There will be so much focus and attention on your relationship, so much tension, that you will not be able to do your job."

The personal advice went, "It's too hard. Why do you want to have any relationship now?" (This was before most of them had met James or seen him in action. After they got to know him it was more like, "How *could* you?")

The objections were pretty strident in the beginning. People would say things like, "How could you go out with a *Democrat?*" Which I always thought was stupid. That's like saying, "I'm a Catholic, how could I go out with a Jew?"

—Mary Matalin, married to
James Carville since 1993

Love alone is capable of uniting living beings in such a way as to complete and fulfill them, for it alone takes them and joins them by what is deepest in themselves.

—Pierre Teilhard de Chardin

The Dance of Love

BY ANNE MORROW LINDBERGH

A good relationship has a pattern like a dance and is built on some of the same rules. The partners do not need to hold on tightly, because they move confidently in the same pattern, intricate but gay and swift and free, like a country dance of Mozart's. To touch heavily would be to arrest the pattern and freeze the movement, to check the endlessly changing beauty of its unfolding. There is no place here for the possessive clutch, the clinging arm, the heavy hand; only the barest touch in passing. Now arm in arm, now face to face, now back to back—it does not matter which. Because they know they are partners moving to the same rhythm, creating a pattern together, and being invisibly nourished by it.

The joy of such a pattern is not only the joy of creation or the joy of participation, it is also the joy of living in the moment. Lightness of touch and living in the moment are intertwined. One cannot dance well unless one is completely in time with the music, not leaning back to the last step or pressing forward to the next one, but poised directly on the present step as it comes. Perfect poise on the beat is what gives good dancing its sense of ease, of timelessness, of the eternal.

Chapter Eight

FRIENDS, LOVERS, AND SOUL MATES

*The rivers of our soul
spring from the same well.*

Chinese poet Po Chü-I

*Everything that touches us,
you and me,
takes us together
like a violin's bow
which draws one voice
out of two separate things.*

—Rainer Maria Rilke

I do believe that fate can put people together who are meant to be together. I do think there's destiny in your life. I think it's true that love brings out the best in us. And that's why we seek it out. That's the way we experience the best of ourselves: by loving somebody else and wanting to be there for them.

—Annette Bening, married to
Warren Beatty since 1992

At Blenheim I took two very important decisions: to be born and marry. I am content with the decision I took on both occasions.

—Winston Churchill

I was born married.

—Bob Hope, married to Dolores for
more than six decades

⌒∞⌒

Familiarity Breeds Content
BY MICHAEL LEACH

Some say familiarity breeds contempt. I have learned that it breeds con*tent*.

When we're content we are satisfied, gratified, and often delighted. We feel warm, comfortable, and cozy. We are at ease. If we're lucky enough to marry the right person—and if we work hard enough to *be* the right person—in time these qualities characterize our marriage as much as crisp air and clear skies typify the beginning of autumn.

Familiarity is knowing someone so well that you both say the same surprising things at the same time, and feel the love in the laughter that follows.

It is being so close to the other that you think her thoughts and feel her feelings at the same time she thinks and feels them.

Familiarity is the comfort of sitting next to the same person at the movies and sharing a soft drink from the same cup for the eight millionth time.

It is pizza together every Friday night.

Familiarity is the assurance of getting a hug just when you need it, and often when you least expect it.

It is the surprising joy of receiving a foot massage, unasked for, while watching TV together.

Familiarity is the thrill of flowers delivered to your office on your anniversary and Valentine's Day—something you're accustomed to but anticipate still.

It is the relaxation that comes from having a golf or tennis partner whom you don't need to impress.

Familiarity is loving the way she walks.

It is liking the way he talks.

Familiarity is gazing at her face and appreciating the beauty that time adds, not takes away.

It is hearing her say that you look the same today as you did when we got married, and knowing it's not true but that she really means it.

Familiarity is having a free fashion consultant.

It is someone who tells you the truth about yourself without hurting you.

Familiarity is confessing your sins to someone who won't be shocked and will still love you and help you see more clearly.

It is never blaming or being blamed, except in jest.

Familiarity is looking at old pictures and sharing the same memories.

It is not caring about taking new pictures but appreciating the present experience as it happens.

Familiarity is doing what the other wants when the other is more passionate about it than you are about what you want to do, like going to a Clint Eastwood movie rather than the new Merchant-Ivory.

It is remembering to get the Merchant-Ivory when it comes out on video.

Familiarity is buying the groceries each Saturday because she never liked doing it.

It is washing the clothes every Sunday because he hates doing that.

Familiarity is no longer arguing about who's the good guy and who's the bad guy when it comes to raising your kids.

It is appreciating your grown children and watching them bloom on their own, in gratitude and awe.

Familiarity is a vacation for two.

It is not needing to leave the country or city or even your home to have a good time.

Familiarity is being alone together, and being together even when you're alone.

Familiarity is being satisfied, gratified, and delighted. It feels warm, comfortable, and cozy.

Familiarity is the sweet fruit of a loving, long-term companionship—a special kind of friendship that breeds content.

It is being at ease.

On this earth who could ask for anything more?

∽∞∾

We're best friends, and we're in this together.

—Faith Hill, married to Tim McGraw
since 1996

I like being married because I want to always be with my best friend. As a child, my best friend and I were inseparable. I never grew out of this, and I don't think anyone does. Now I can be with my best friend every day, share my secrets with him, laugh together, share wonderful memories together, support each other, grow together, and live together.

—Ellie Flores
San Diego, California

cᴓᴐ

One Long Conversation

BY JAMES M. SOMERVILLE AND BEATRICE BRUTEAU

We used to say that if we earned a nickel for every minute we spent in philo-sophical/spiritual conversation, we'd be rich. But, of course, the conversa-tion itself is the true wealth. It's been going on since we first met in 1955 and is still as full of excitement and discovery as ever. Probably more so, be-cause we know more now. There are more ideas to bring into collision or collusion with one another and less timidity about tracing and facing the implications.

It's great way to stay alive. Keeps you young. During the year 2001 Jim was eighty-five and Beatrice was seventy. Our late marriage did not result in the gift of children but we believe it has been fruitful in its own way, and it could be that our experience will encourage others in a similar situation. Having common interests is a big help. One of the pleasures of our lives has been the joy of "finding things out," to quote Richard Feynman; learning to distinguish between truth and illusion, exchanging ideas, sometimes dis-agreeing, then reaching a final resolution. So we have been reading, dis-cussing, publishing, and teaching for almost fifty years.

While our main work has been in the areas of philosophy and religion, science looms large in our lives because that is where the mystery of being in the finite world is unveiled. Einstein said that he just wanted to know how the Old One (God) thinks. What can be more exhilarating than to find out how things work in the cosmological, chemical, and biological world! And in the human world to drink in the wonder of classical music and appreciate the work of our artist friends.

Just to be alive is such a gift. And every day there is something new to learn. So we teach one another, communicating what we know best. Beatrice is the scientist and mystical theologian, Jim the poet, scripture scholar, and linguist. Never a dull moment. When there are no guests, we read to each other at mealtime; it's almost monastic. One reads while the other eats, and we interrupt for discussion. One day Beatrice has found a better book on the global economy or the Jewish renewal movement. Jim shares his latest findings in biblical archeology or a neat paragraph from

Philo's *Logos*. Beatrice comes back with an article on the Higgs particle which may be substantiated by a powerful accelerator in Switzerland. For "dessert" we often laugh at the humorous stories of P. G. Wodehouse, or Jim recites one of his limericks on the great philosophers of the West:

> *Now it might be presumptuous to paint*
> *The doubting Descartes as a saint,*
> *But he always insisted*
> *He really existed*
> *'Cause you can't think you aren't if you ain't!*

On the first day of the new millennium (2001) we celebrated the forty-sixth anniversary of the day we first met on the sidewalk in front of the library at Fordham University, where we were both employed. Many joint projects later, we still rise each morning to add one more day to a friendship that grows in mutual admiration and devotion.

We are drawing close to the fiftieth year of this long conversation. We have been fortunate in keeping pace with one another, finding ourselves in agreement as we develop from one stage to another. We enjoy the same things, especially new ideas, life here in the country, shared political and social concerns, mutual friends. There's still so much to learn, to enjoy. We're grateful and hope to go on for a long while together.

It's good to have someone to talk to!

James M. Somerville and Beatrice Bruteau, founders of Schola Contemplationis, an international community of contemplatives, have been married since 1971.

∽

A happy marriage is a long conversation that always seems too short.
—André Malraux

When marrying, ask yourself this question: Do you believe that you will be able to converse with this person into your old age? Everything else in marriage is transitory.
—Friedrich Nietzsche

⤫

The Magic Touch

BY VALERIE SCHULTZ

At age nine, I had an epiphany. I was watching my parents holding hands as we walked across a parking lot after a football game. It was late afternoon, and they were in front of me, their silhouettes tilted toward each other intimately. It was a jolt: the first time I perceived them as something separate from me. They were my parents, but now I saw that they were also a couple, a man and a woman who had fallen in love and whose happiness was captured in those black-and-white wedding photos and who still loved each other enough to hold hands on an autumn afternoon.

Now I am the mother, and I've been caught. "Close your eyes," my 11-year-old tells my 8-year-old. "Mom and Dad are kissing in the kitchen again." Of course they both watch us, giggling from behind their masks of fingers. When they can't stand it anymore, they hop onto our backs. They want their kisses, too. My husband and I kiss in the kitchen, we kiss in the hallway, and sometimes we even make out on the front porch. I believe it's healthy for us to kiss in front of our children. It's good for them, like fresh air and clean clothes. It helps them grow in tender and nurturing ways.

As much as I think of us as a couple in love, albeit four daughters later, our children see us as their parents first. The dawning realization that we have a separate identity as man and woman comes at different ages. I know our two older children's initial reaction to learning how babies are made was to picture Mom and Dad doing such a ludicrous thing. "No way!" they said, "Not my parents!" (Or, as a friend's child said with a sweet smile upon learning the mechanics of sex: "I think I'll adopt.") Now I imagine that, as teenagers, they are faintly repulsed at the idea that we "do it." Our middle-schooler, on the cusp of many things, regards us thoughtfully as she works things out. Our youngest still knows we are entirely hers.

Our children have never caught us in the act, I'm happy to say. There was a close call years ago, when, just as we were catching our breath, a light shone in our eyes. It was the beam of a circus flashlight, a gift that day from Grandpa, followed by a weaving, half-asleep child making her way to our bedroom. No police spotlight could ever seem brighter than that flashlight did. After that we locked our bedroom door.

Although it's possible that our children have heard us making love, we take our precautions. We check on young sleepers. We say goodnight to teenagers holed up in their rooms, music safely blaring. We close our curtains, light the candles, check the door lock again and attack each other. In some ways we are like wayward teenagers ourselves, sneaking around, having surreptitious sex, giddily celebrating the rarely empty house. But while our lovemaking is discreet, our physical affection for each other is not. Our children have grown up with the awareness that we dig each other.

Married sex continually delights with its intimacy, its innovation, its deepening appreciation for the physical gift of the other. It becomes more pleasurable with time, trust and love. It's easy to buy into the advertising line that sex is only for the young and beautiful. But the better portion secretly belongs to us: the faithfully married, even with our deepening lines and softer bellies, our visible veins and the gray threads in our hair. Yes, there are dry spells, when life is so busy that we collapse into bed exhausted. We don't have time for sex, as it's not on the to-do list. But sooner or later it makes its way to the top of the list, as we drop everything and feast on each other. Then we realize why we've been so grumpy lately. Why don't we do this more often? we ask. It is a question with no good answer.

We are touchers; we are huggers. We hold hands when we walk. Our touching is an expanding circle. We snuggle and smooch our kids. Our teenagers can only handle a brief arm around their shoulders without embarrassment. But this parental touch is just as important as inhaling their baby-sweet necks used to be. A child who is loved and touched affectionately at home is less likely to seek physical gratification elsewhere.

We touch, we love. We have four vivid, beautiful daughters, the fruit of the power of this awesome thing we do with God. Are we role models for their future relationships? I hope so. And I hope the old adage about looking for someone just like dear old Dad is not far from the truth. I could wish them no greater joy than the magic of a touchable marriage.

My parents are soon to celebrate their 50th wedding anniversary. The waters of joy and sorrow, of success and disappointment, of anger and forgiveness have flowed mightily under their bridge. Yet along their journey, their touches of love have enthralled, have soothed, have healed.

My parents are my daughters' history and roots. My daughters are my parents' hope and affirmation. My daughters think their grandparents are adorable as they share their vitamins at the breakfast table and correct each other's stories of long ago, of the Navy and hard times and their first baby daughter.

I notice that they walk more slowly. They still hold hands.

Valerie Schultz, wife and mother, writes from Tehachapi, California.

⌀

Wild Nights—Wild Nights!
Were I with thee
Wild Nights should be
Our luxury!

Futile—the Winds—
To a Heart in port—
Done with the Compass—
Done with the Chart!

Rowing in Eden—
Ah, the Sea!
Might I but moor—Tonight—
In thee!

—Emily Dickinson

There is no place like a bed for confidential disclosures between friends. Man and wife, they say, there open the very bottoms of their souls to each other; and some old couples often lie and chat over old times till nearly morning.

—Herman Melville, *Moby-Dick*

Sex is an errant stroke of God's most choice lightning—wild horse beyond control—its own excuse for being; having no allegiance, playing by its own rules with loaded dice. Love, on the other hand, is the maker—and keeper—of our humanity, to be trusted above all other instincts, nurtured, worked at, molded, shaped, then remolded . . . a garden where we labor against rocks which in time become flowers; one life held in common, rosebush, thorns, and all. But marriage is the place which love calls home.

—Ossie Davis, married to Ruby Dee
since 1948

You meet somebody that attracts your eye. First comes the physical attraction. Then you begin to feel that you need that person. My marriage has lasted because the need has persisted. And it's also, you know, from time to time—the other thing.

—Carroll O'Connor, married to Nancy
from 1951 until his death in 2001

When you have a family and children, private time becomes very important, so you have to try to sneak it in the best you can. I have three daughters and they take up a lot of focus and time. When Marivi and I have spontaneous romantic moments, they have a spirit that sort of lingers. So we don't have to have them every single moment of the day.

—Andy Garcia, married to Marivi Garcia
since 1982

Making Room for Someone Else
BY KATHLEEN WALSH

My parents had two favorite marriage proverbs that they happily reiterated (without any prompting) many times over. The first was that marriage isn't a 50/50 proposition, but a 100/100 one. Both persons have to give everything to make the partnership work. Their other oft-repeated axiom was this: Love is a decision. Despite the fact that they uttered these with the best of intentions, I always found that their well-meaning advice seemed to drain all the romance out of things. It was almost as if you got married and then rolled up your sleeves and settled in for a lifetime of drudgery in order to make this sketchy proposition last.

When I fell in love with my husband, I didn't feel as if I had to decide anything. It was clear and easy: I loved him and always would. We had something special going for us; we were on each other's "wavelength"; we were, in essence "soul mates." But after the honeymoon passed and his endearing habits became minor annoyances (as did mine, I'm sure), I realized what my parents had tried, somewhat unsuccessfully, to communicate. Marriage isn't keeping tabs on who did what and how much so as to keep all things equal, but about giving all that you have lavishly and without condition. Marriage is about deciding each moment to act with love, to say the loving word and to make the loving gesture, even when you're tired or aggravated or just simply sick of making the effort.

I think the concept of soul mates has less to do with finding some kind of idealized soul mate than with making a decision to make your mate a part of your very soul. Before I met my husband I wasn't sure I could be that vulnerable with another person. I was always kind of private and had doubts about the wisdom of opening myself up too much. And, on the flip side, I wondered if I could really undertake the gentle but demanding responsibility of caring for another's heart. I worried that I didn't have the patience or the energy it would require.

But we worked at it. It wasn't always easy, and it wasn't all forward progress. There were times I thought I was living with an alien and he thought I was a raving lunatic. Gradually, though, we learned about giving 100 percent and about deciding to love and about finding the energy and patience and about becoming vulnerable. And we learned because of each other, not in spite of each other. Mostly, we learned that we could be more, give more, and love more than we had thought.

I can turn to him for strength when I feel mine begin to waver—and know he will keep me going. And he can lean on me when he needs to and knows that I will be there without question. He's enormously patient and kind, and he makes numerous tiny gestures each day to let me know how important I am to him. And I remind him all the time of how great I think he is and how he has made my life richer and more joyful.

Being a soul mate is work, yes, but not some sort of deadening routine. It's about stretching yourself—your heart and soul—to become something more than you had been. Being a soul mate, in essence, is about making room in the deepest part of yourself for someone else and entrusting the other person with a part of yourself in return.

Kathleen Walsh lives in Mahwah, New Jersey, and has been married to Joe DeAngelo since 1993.

⁓∞⁓

Our engagement took place in the simplest way, without any proposal. We were alone in my parents' living room. Jacques was sitting on the rug, close to my chair; it suddenly seemed to me that we had always been near each other, and that we would always be so. Without thinking, I put out my hand and stroked his hair; he looked at me and all was clear to us. The feeling flowed through me that always . . . my life would be bound up with Jacques'. It was one of those tender and peaceful feelings which are like a gift flowing from a region higher than ourselves, illuminating the future and deepening the present. From that moment our understanding was perfect and unchangeable.

> —Raïssa Maritain, married to Jacques
> from 1904 until her death in 1960

Whatever our souls are made of, his and mine are the same.
> —Emily Brontë, *Wuthering Heights*

From every human being there rises a light that reaches straight to heaven, and when two souls that are destined to be together find each other their streams of light flow together and a single, brighter light goes forth from their united being.
> —Baal Shem Tov

A successful marriage requires falling in love many times, always with the same person.
> —Mignon McLaughlin

Husband and wife come to look alike at last.
> —Oliver Wendell Holmes

Forgiveness

People ask me what advice I have for a married couple struggling in their relationship. I always answer: pray and forgive.
                                                    —Mother Teresa of Calcutta

Forgiveness is not blaming.
                                                    —Thomas Hora, M.D.

Without forgiveness, love has no meaning. It has no fullness or maturity. Only when two people have shown each other the worst side of our natures are we truly ready for the task of love. Then we're ready to begin. How tragic it is that so often we stop everything just as we reach the starting line.
                                                    —Marianne Williamson

Melissa sees the real me—my strengths and weaknesses, my best and my very worst. She likes the best and has forgiven the worst. That kind of unconditional love and acceptance has bonded our marriage.
                                                    —Tom Lehman, married to Melissa
                                                    since 1987

That goes both ways, of course.
                                                    —Melissa Lehman

A happy marriage is the union of two good forgivers.
                                                    —Ruth Bell Graham

People are always asking couples whose marriages have endured at least a quarter of a century for their secret for success. Actually, it's no secret at all. I am a forgiving woman. Long ago, I forgave my husband for not being Paul Newman.

—Erma Bombeck

Chapter Nine

IN GOOD TIMES AND BAD

A friend knows the song
in my heart
and sings it to me
when my memory fails.

unknown

I am a nurse and care for people who are fighting cancer. It is amazing to witness the hope of people who have the support of their spouses in contrast to those without family support. Having someone unconditionally by your side for life is a wonderful feeling. At work, I witness the strong bond of marriage when the spouse of an ill person sits by their side and actually gives them the will to survive and the strength to fight, as well as peace and serenity. This is a gift that cannot be bought and it can only be given out of love and marriage. Chris and I married three years ago because we wanted to demonstrate to each other exactly how much we love one another. Marriage is the ultimate gift of love.

—Ellie Flores
San Diego, California

Love often makes itself visible in pain.

—Henri J. M. Nouwen

Dana came into the room. She stood beside me, and we made eye contact. I mouthed my first lucid words to her: "Maybe we should let me go." Dana started crying. She said, "I am only going to say this once: I will support whatever you want to do, because this is your life, and your decision. But I want you to know that I'll be with you for the long haul, no matter what." Then she added the words that saved my life: "You're still you. And I love you."

If she had looked away or paused or hesitated even slightly, or if I had felt there was a sense of her being—being what?—noble, or fulfilling some obligation to me, I don't know if I could have pulled through. Because it had dawned on me that I was going to be a huge burden to everybody, that I had ruined my life and everybody else's. Not fair to anybody. The best thing to do would be to slip away.

But what Dana said made living seem possible, because I felt the depth of her love and commitment. I was even able to make a little joke. I mouthed, "This is way beyond the marriage vows—in sickness and in health." And she said, "I know." I knew then and there that she was going to be with me forever.

—Christopher Reeve, married to
Dana since 1992

Hearts will never be practical until they are made unbreakable.

—The Wizard of Oz

The only thing in life that is truly whole is a broken heart.

—Baal Shem Tov

CRSO

Little Miracle

BY EVANDER AND FOTINI LOMKE

The world stopped on April 19, 1990.

Our world.

Our bright, curly haired three-and-a-half-year-old Elizabeth closed her eyes and slumped. It was like the sound of a silent crash. For us, an eternity passed in the span of twenty minutes. Little did we know how much our lives could change over lunch.

It happened between pediatric appointments, in a hospital cafeteria— no shortage of doctors there. One would eventually tell us that Elizabeth had a seizure. "She may have epilepsy. It's a disorder not all that unusual in children. It's often outgrown. But medication will have to be taken as a precaution. If she has no other seizures after a certain length of time, the medication can be eliminated."

What? We hardly knew what epilepsy was. It typically runs in families. Neither of us had any such history.

The medication turned out to be a disaster of side effects and worsening conditions. Others were tried. Combinations. Injectable steroids. Something called the ketogenic diet, a seemingly grotesque regimen of high-fat consumption. We felt as if we had gone through the looking glass. But if it would help . . . Unfortunately, the seizures became much more intense and frequent. Treatments made things worse. Specialists of every sort were consulted. A degenerative disease was suspected, then ruled out. AIDS was a possibility, though we couldn't imagine how. The testing was often painful, including a bone-marrow procedure and biopsies. The doctors began looking for diseases too rare and hideous to name.

Finally, a week before Christmas, a diagnosis was made by the hospital's chief of pediatric neurology: Lennox-Gastaut syndrome, one of the most brutal forms of epilepsy. Even neurologists don't come across it very often. We learned there are 50,000 of these cases— Is that in the United States or the world? Did it matter? Elizabeth's IQ dropped 90 points: profound retardation as a result of countless petit mal and grand mal seizures. Now four years old, she could neither walk nor talk anymore. Because of the seizures,

Elizabeth's sleep was often by fits and starts. How exhausted we all were. Nothing could be counted on now. Oh, we did know one thing: we wouldn't need that college fund anymore.

What had Elizabeth done to deserve this fate? What would become of our little family? Could this be a cross too heavy to be ours?

As the years passed, the few ups and the many downs of this strange, disabling condition kept us on our toes. The seizures made it difficult for Elizabeth to do much of anything. The harder she tried to concentrate when we read to her, the more seizures she had. Some caused her to cry and scream. One unusual seizure made her shut her eyes and not open them for the longest time. And once in a while a seizure caused her to stop breathing and turn blue, which required oxygen immediately. Until better forms of treatment came along, we continued to be regulars at the ER. A bag was always packed in anticipation. One Thanksgiving was spent in the children's ward. Another year, it was Christmas. Some friends, especially those with healthier small children, contacted us less and less often. In their good times, we learned, people don't want to be reminded of the ever-present possibility of the bad.

But we survived, and the self-questioning is now largely a thing of the past. Yet, after all this time, other, bigger questions remain. How did this soul, with such an extraordinary condition, find two such ordinary people as we? Why us? Why on earth?

Before Elizabeth was born, a good friend told us that children in heaven choose their parents. We wonder. We were married for ten years when Elizabeth had that first seizure. We have now been married twenty. "These situations put a strain on a marriage." "Get counseling!" "There are permanent institutions for such children." "Say, I know a couple whose child . . . and do you know how *they* ended up?"

Many people do mean well. But no matter how well-intentioned or how hard they try, when you find yourself living in a unique situation, and are actually *wedded* to it—when the getting through each day amounts to another in a line of unexpected blessings just by having made it through the evening—no person outside of ourselves can really understand or be of help. The years have taught us a new way to live; each of us has learned acceptance and new ways to grow.

Our faith has been tested. So has our will. They still are! Even more than most, we haven't a clue what tomorrow brings. Life follows a script that the living cannot read. But being in a medically guarded condition forces us to confront, and focus on, the plotless, precious present. Elizabeth, and our expectations for her, started out one way. She is now blossoming in another. Although still nonverbal, wheelchair-bound, and completely dependent on us and others for all her needs, she is a beautiful teen with the spark of life in her eyes. To us, she is the sun, the moon, and the stars. We couldn't imagine our lives together any other way.

Elizabeth Lomke—"Little Miracle."
PHOTO BY CONNIE PAPOULAS.

Evander Lomke is a vice president and managing editor of Continuum International. **Fotini Lomke** is a parent member in the New York City special-education preschool program and is an advocate for the rights of disabled children. They have been married since 1980.

⬥

Where there is great love, there are always miracles.
—Willa Cather

In every human being there is a special heaven, whole and unbroken.
—Paracelsus

When I told her [about having Parkinson's disease] . . . she didn't panic. She didn't draw back. I could tell immediately that she was in [this with me for the long haul], and then it was okay, we'll deal with it. It's led me on a terrific journey of looking at things. And I would

not be as happy a person today were it not for this journey that I've
been on.

—Michael J. Fox, married to
Tracy Pollan since 1988

For those few years, [Joy] and I feasted on love; every mode of it—
solemn and merry, romantic and realistic, sometimes as dramatic as
a thunderstorm, sometimes as comfortable and unemphatic as putting on your soft slippers.

—C. S. Lewis

Above all things, my father valued his marriage and his family. He
taught me how to be a good husband to my wife and a dedicated
father to my children.

When Dad died I felt a terrible emptiness. I sensed I was alone
in a very deep way. Standing by his hospital bed, I made an immediate call to my wife, who had been waiting by the phone for word
on his condition. "Anne," I said, "I don't have a father anymore."

In uttering those painful words to her, I realized that the commitment we made to each other on our wedding day, "I will love
you in good times and in bad," was a lifeline for me. Anne was the
only person I wanted to talk to, the only person in the entire world
who would understand my sense of loss. And she gave me the love
and support I needed at a moment when I felt an expanding hole
in my heart.

That natural selflessness, along with many other acts of kindness in marriage, is one mark of a committed spouse, a true soul
mate. A friend of mine once said, "Breathe heaven and heavenly
things will be yours." As my father took his last breath he allowed
me to fill my lungs with the heavenly air of my wife's love. I miss
him still, but for that I will always be grateful.

—Jack Kernion
Wexford, Pennsylvania

My heart sickens at all the sadness in the sweet,
the sweetness in the sad.

—Francis Thompson

There comes a moment to everyone
When Beauty stands staring into the soul
With sad sweet eyes
That sicken at the sound of words.
And God help those who pass that moment by.

—Edmond Rostand, *Cyrano de Bergerac*, Act III

⚮

One Day at a Time
BY SIDNEY CALLAHAN

I never dreamed that I would start all over mothering a baby girl at age sixty-three. Dan and I had raised five sons and a daughter, now in their mid-thirties and forties. But tragedy befell our family four years ago. Thirty hours after the birth of our son Peter's baby, her mother died in the hospital. An unsuspected blood clot in Ann's leg migrated to her lungs and she suffocated in panic and pain. Death struck just as she had fulfilled her lifelong desire to become a mother. In an instant our family moved from celebration to shock and grief, stumbling into a future forever changed. My husband and I flew to Los Angeles and brought our son and his newborn daughter, Perry Ann, to our home in New York where we all began to cope—one day at a time.

I had always wanted to be a grandmother but never under such tragic circumstances. It had been so long since all my children had left home. Beginning again was a dreadful adjustment. Many things about baby care had changed. My daughter Sarah had just had her first son two months before Perry's birth so she was my expert advisor. We reversed roles as I called her up frantically for advice. "Mom," she would say, "relax. Babies get colds, you know." I launched into the first of a series of new-mother talks with the young about pacifiers, sleeping problems, potty training, and choosing nursery schools. One question kept coming to my mind: How did I ever do this before? And why with so many?

Even as a child I longed for a large family. My younger sister and I were often lonely and always looked forward to visiting our numerous cousins and Southern relatives. In adolescence I dreamt myself at the head of a table of six children, four of them girls, just like the mother in *Little Women*. My tendencies toward procreative plenitude were typical of the domestic '50s, of course, but my particular visions were abetted by the biblical promise to Abraham that his descendants would be numerous as the stars. My great-grandfather had been a foot-washing Baptist minister in south Alabama and had eighteen children—nine by the first wife and nine by the second. Big families sounded like so much fun, as well as being fruitful.

Dan and I married at a youthful twenty-four and twenty-one. He proposed that we aim for twelve children (the movie that played in his mind was *Cheaper by the Dozen*). I protested that I could only manage a modest family of six because I wanted to have a career. My plan was to have six children by the time I was thirty, get a Ph.D. by thirty-five, and then teach at a college in my forties. Why not?

Newly married in 1954 we embarked on achieving our first goals, getting Dan through graduate school on the G.I. Bill—and producing babies. Our morale was high, much as young recruits rush into an exhilarating military campaign. Dan battled with the Harvard philosophy department, and lived at the library. I struggled to survive in the slums of Cambridge. I had one baby in a charity ward and found out firsthand how badly poor women are treated.

After we had produced four baby boys in six years, it seemed like a good idea for Dan to take a job in New York City as an editor of *Commonweal* magazine—so we could eat while he finished his dissertation. We now made enough money to actually pay taxes and buy a small house in Hastings-on-Hudson, a river town suburb where we have lived ever since. Middle-class status had arrived, and not a moment too soon. In fact, while coping with penury had been hard, other things happened which took much more prayer and divine help to survive. The great family trauma of those early years was losing our fourth baby son, Thomas, in a sudden infant crib death on my twenty-eighth birthday. Looking back I can see that I was very depressed, not only by the loss of our baby but by moving away from supportive friends. But in those days we knew nothing of the process of grieving and bereavement. We were suspicious of psychology, and had no thought of getting any help for our three surviving boys or ourselves. We just pushed on, one day at a time, and as soon as possible had three more babies in three years, one of which to our surprise was a little girl. Now I had my six children and the full-court press for intellectual and family productivity continued.

Along about this time however, I grew frustrated in our isolated suburban setting and took up an offer from a publishing friend. He suggested that I might write a book as Dan had already done. The topic would be the new challenges women face. It would combine faith and feminism in a new synthesis. I had never thought of becoming a writer, but since I couldn't afford to go to graduate school, writing could provide an intellectual outlet. Hiring a baby-sitter with my $300 advance, I wrote for two hours a day, like Virginia Woolf. Unlike her, however, I had to take time out to nurse and clear piles of laundry off my bedroom table-desk. Somehow, the manuscript was at last delivered, and the book, *The Illusion of Eve,* came out to great fanfare in 1965—as did our last child.

During the next decades Dan and I pursued more writing projects and our careers flourished. Dan founded the Hastings Center, a bioethical research institute, without any assured funding. This was a creative act of risk-taking but we had been prepared by past acts of adventure. Gradually, I went to graduate school part time and in stages and finally received a Ph.D., in psychology no less (my B.A. in English was in 1955, *magna cum baby*), and the doctorate was awarded in 1980. We always tried to involve the children in our activities and take them with us on lecture engagements when we could. We experienced good times, as individuals and as a family.

Things changed in the late '60s and '70s when we found ourselves blindsided by the social and sexual revolution. We raised our teenagers in the midst of Vietnam War protests, student riots, the hippie movement, assassinations, crises in the church and schools, and last but not least, the arrival of drugs and the sexual revolution in our own town. In retrospect it seemed as though one year our children were attending dancing classes and church in coats and ties, and the next year all hell broke loose. Young people in town rebelled, turned on, dropped out, grew their hair, asserted their sexual freedom, and sometimes overdosed and died. Certain sophisticated parents in our suburb also went crazy, smoking pot and approving sexual liberation (i.e., promiscuity) for themselves and their adolescent children. Dan and I felt as though our family had been run over by a steamroller. Cultural forces we could not control were stronger than we were, no matter how hard we struggled.

We suffered, along with our children. Their rebellions punctured my maternal pride but my parental concern for their welfare grew even stronger. Fighting for the soul and safety of adolescents made everything I had ever done before seem easy. Like many parents of our generation we experienced a decade of difficulty we never could have imagined. Living through the troubles was a test of love; only faith kept me from giving up hope.

But even during the tough times we had wonderful experiences as a family. Affection, humor, and lively conversation were as much a part of our home as leaky faucets, dirty diapers, and clunky radiators. Our children were smart, social, and athletic, if not spiritual and high achievers at school. Our house was always jumping. I insisted on cooking them breakfast every morning (a way to get them up and out) and on being together at family dinner every night. Although I taught Sunday school, I gave up trying to enforce church attendance. At home, however, I continued my subtle, and not so subtle, missionary efforts for civilization, literature, and the faith. I enjoyed talking to our children's friends (also a way to find out more about what my children were up to) and welcomed them in Southern style. Our house was always full.

As they went to college, Dan and I envisioned a new time when we would grow together as two again. In time all of our children blossomed into responsible adults and left the nest. Dan and I enjoyed this new peaceful period. As a companionable older couple we began to exercise more, and regularly walk and play tennis together in an ongoing effort to stay in good physical shape. And a good thing too, for stamina became the most valued resource when the 1996 tragedy arrived.

On March 6, on my sixty-third birthday, adorable baby Perry was born. I was overcome at the coincidence of having joy and sorrow celebrated on the same day. Ann's death prompted an outpouring of love and care from our family, friends, and neighbors. Everyone touched by the sad event wanted to do something, anything, to help. Suffering gives human beings an opportunity to care for one other.

I have to admit, however, that even with support (and enough money to get the help of a full-time nanny), part of me doubted that I would be able to make it through. Being cast back into the responsible role of nurturing an infant at home produced bouts of anxiety and exhaustion. And despite all my adoration of this wonderful baby, I did not possess the same physical energy or confidence of my youth. My work also suffered since I was so tired all the time. I resolved this incipient feeling of resentment by quitting my teaching position at Mercy College in order to spend my free time writing. Ironically, I am back to a desk in my bedroom, since our empty-nest apartment has become completely stuffed. But I like being a full-time writer and an active residential grandma.

My major task now is a mothering one for Perry, as well as to be a good grandmother to my daughter's boys and a supportive mother to all of our adult children. The roles of wife and caretaker-daughter to my ninety-year-old mother and eighty-eight-year-old stepmother are also new challenges. Now that Perry is almost five and going to school, the role of the team, daddy, grandpa, and grandma, is becoming easier.

And what joy and light our granddaughter Perry has brought to Dan and myself! We feel bonded in our love and care for her, just as we did the first time around as young parents. It helps that she is a blithe spirit, a star, a princess, a Shirley Temple enchantress. While I sometimes suffer charm fatigue, my heart has been enlarged. Moreover, I have been forced to pray more regularly, become more disciplined and ascetic, and generally nourish my body and spirit. What better way to enter into the third act of this drama than one day at a time, just as always?

Thanksgiving and Christmas are coming. Like the mother in *Little Women,* I will sit at that table surrounded by my husband, our children, their spouses, their significant others, and my beautiful grandchildren.

My spirit rejoices!

Sidney Callahan is a psychologist, a columnist for *Commonweal* magazine, and an author whose books include the award-winning *With All*

Sidney and Perry: Life begins again.

Our Heart and Mind: The Spiritual Works of Mercy in a Psychological Age. She and Dan have been married since 1954.

⌒∞ͻ

Do you know what you are? You are a marvel. In all the world there is no other exactly like you.
—Pablo Casals

I am very fortunate to have Noor by my side. The most wonderful part of our relationship is the amount of care, concern and support in this rather difficult time.
—King Hussein of Jordan, married to Queen Noor from 1978 until his death in 1999

I think I'm a much better person for having known and loved him.
—Queen Noor

Good marriages don't just happen; they take a lot of love and a lot of work. When things get rough, you don't just cut and run.
—Tipper Gore, married to Al since 1970

We believe in like at first sight, even lust at first sight. One glance can make your hormones go snap, crackle and pop. But love is a bit more complicated. We've been married 32 years, and in love a lot longer than that. It's our experience that love takes time and tears, joy and loss. Love is based on sharing and respect, not just chemistry. Strolling on a starlit beach, holding hands and planning for the future, is a loving experience. But so is sitting at the bedside of an ailing parent, holding hands and remembering the past. The key is staying connected and committed, day after day. That's real love.
—Cokie and Steve Roberts, married since 1966

We should measure affection not like youngsters, by the ardor of its passion, but by its strength and constancy.
                                    —Cicero

⟨∞⟩

Staying Together
BY RUBY DEE

Love, marriage, relationships, staying together—ain't easy. I was looking into the eager young face of a woman after one of our performances on a campus, when I found myself trying to articulate what I really felt about marital longevity besides "Don't go to bed angry," or "You've just got to keep God in the equation," or "Try to remain attractive to each other." Ossie and I *had* gone through some rough times. Emotions that affect most married people—resentment, anger, impatience, jealousy—had affected us, too. How to ride the rough waves in a relationship long enough for the waters to get calm? When does it sink in that overcoming difficult times gets easier with practice? How do you drag some of the good feelings, good times vibrations into the stormy places? To love someone long and deep is a "consummation devoutly to be wished!"

This letter to Ossie is an effort to put something about love and marriage under a microscope and into at least some elementary perspective.

Dear Ossie,

I appreciate and acknowledge the fact that you are a good husband. For a while, though, I believed that a truly nice husband could not be achieved without a lot of hard work—if the sista is lucky and the brotha is intelligent and flexible. That such creatures couldn't even be born is due perhaps to some trauma in the birthing process of your gender. After the first several of our fifty years together, I was convinced of it. The idea that a good marriage is made in heaven and swung down on a golden cord like a gift from God did not coincide with my lifelong observations. Yes, the wedding can be a beautiful, exciting, expensive event, or it can be a handshake, or a jump over a broom—but it is just that—an event, the one that precedes the marriage.

I maintain, however, that this oneness, this coming together under one roof "until death do us part" is a challenging proposition. Unlike the wedding event that takes place in a day, marriage is a long process that goes on at some level every day for the rest of your life. You divorce or marry around some issue constantly. The percentage of days married determines success. We have to *learn* how to live together. Oh, well. That shouldn't be too tough if you love somebody.

I thought I loved you, Ossie, when we got married, but as I see now, I was only in the kindergarten of the proposition. To arrive at love is like working on a double doctorate in the subject of Life. . . .

Breakfast became more than just a time for food. We eventually learned how to pray together every day, even if only by phone. I don't remember when current political, economic, and social matters became our favorite topics, but I do remember how they stimulated us, especially you. How you love history, and cross-referencing and comparison. How, when the children were very young, you told stories and jokes, and spread your spirit over me, too, like a warm blanket on a cold night. How the newspapers and magazines would accumulate because there was so much to catch up on, and to share. More and more, you and I became part of the Struggle and the Struggle became a part of us. . . .

I have admired your capacity to interrelate, to see the long arc of events, sometimes in awesome detail, marrying the mundane and the majestic, the beginnings reflected in the ends. As I listened, I reminded myself again how deeply I love you. Not only because I believe you value me, but also because I believe we have both arrived, finally, at what love is. When you want and pray for someone to be all God created them to be, despite any personal sacrifice it might entail, that is love. Love is overcoming. Love is passion clothed in infinite patience.

There is a magnetism about those who love, who know things, who see, make connections, and are committed to the struggles for the wider victories in the world. There is a sensuousness about them, too—as if struggle itself is an aphrodisiac. During your

Manley address, the silence in the place was so loud. I felt you walking in my secret soul, and that night we had to make love.

Ruby Dee, actress and human rights activist, has been married to Ossie Davis since 1948.

∝

You can tell a good, surviving marriage by the expression in the partners' eyes—like those of sailors who have shared the battles against foul weather—and the scented airs of summer at sea. They welcome visitors—but are content with their own company.
                    —Pam Brown

The course of true love never did run smooth.
                    —William Shakespeare

Listen, in every marriage there's a moment. In every marriage there are a bunch of moments. Horrible, hurtful, I-don't-know-if-I-can-stand-one-more-minute-of-this-pain moments. But you get through them. You get through them because fundamentally your inners know there is something worth salvaging. That your tolerance may be frayed, and your goodwill somewhat eroded, and your passion may have definitely taken a sabbatical—but that in spite of all that, there is much that is worthwhile. There is history, and shared values, and a mutual delight in the miracle that two such intractable people have kept this thing together so far, and that is well worth the effort to continue doing so. Because of one thing, because you believe fiercely in *the worthiness of the imperfect union*.

It's not considered a particularly fashionable thing to believe in these days. Not nearly as fashionable as intimacy, nurturing, et al. Witness a conversation I recently had with an old friend. She was telling me about a new book project. I asked her what it was on. It was, she said, on couples who had been together in long-term marriages. I said, Oh, you mean like old Marlon and me?

Sort of, she said. But particularly marriages in which there had been a lot of *growth*.

Growth? Oh God. Listen, when it comes to marriage, my personal feeling is that "growth" is a four-letter word.

When it comes to marriage, I believe there's a whole lot to be said for "endure."

Nor for endure at any price. But for endure if at all possible. I hope it's possible for Marlon and me. Because true as it is that you only get married for the first time once, it's also true that you only get divorced for the first time once.

And I hear that one's a bitch too.

—Judy Markey
Chicago, Illinois

I like being married because it's demanding—a challenge—you can never totally let up. It's a new parade going by each day. Being single is half a loop—being married completes the circle. It also requires you to develop new talents and new perspectives to deal with compatibility issues that change by the minute.

—Bob Elliott
Greenwich, Connecticut

Love's a mess and I enjoy that mess.

—Sean Penn, married to Robin Wright
since 1996

I want to make a toast. Someday soon you'll have a family of your own. You'll remember the little moments—like this—that were good.

—Tony Soprano, *The Sopranos,* at dinner
with Carmela, Meadow, and Anthony Jr.
at the end of bad day

Bad times pass, but the good times do, too, so savor the good ones as deeply as you can. I hope you and John will always enjoy the now, will always be aware of all the good things that both of you are blessed with: youth and health and friends and energy and hope. Try to remember that little poem I've always loved:

Yesterday is history;
Tomorrow is a mystery.
Today is God's gift;
That's why it's called the Present.

—Joan Rivers (written to her daughter
Melissa on the eve of her wedding)

Zen Mom

BY POLLY BERRIEN BERENDS

Child: Mom, how come you know so much about God?

Mother: I don't know so much. But I have been around for a while and been to many schools and studied with many teachers. There were Moses and Isaiah and Jesus and Buddha. There were many books and professors, and Dr. Hora. But besides all those I have two private Zen masters who are always teaching me and making my learning into real understanding and love. I am very, very grateful for them.

Children: Tell us! Who are they? What are their names? You never told us about them!

Mother: Their names are Jan and Andy. It is you who are my masters.

Children [laughing]: Oh, Mom! *We* teach *you*? You're joking!

Mother: No, I am not kidding. You are my two wonderful Zen masters.

⁕

I really learned it all from mothers.

—Dr. Benjamin Spock

Chapter Ten

ALL IN THE FAMILY

*We are all meant to be mothers of God
for God is always needing to be born.*

—Meister Eckhart

A contented wife and mother is who I am. It's not much of an acting stretch.

> —Rita Wilson, married to Tom Hanks
> since 1988

My family is the reason I live, not the work. You could bring Olivier back from the dead and have him perform Hamlet and I would be at home with my family. The best thing that ever happened to me was getting married. Tracy and [our children] put everything in perspective.

—Michael J. Fox, married to Tracy Pollan
since 1988

After forty-eight years of marriage—babies, diapers, fevers, scouts, tuition, and weddings—I have decided that grandchildren are the greatest reward for a job well done. We spent the last Christmas season with our five children, spouses, and eleven grandchildren. It was wild and wonderful.

—Joan Pettiti
St. Pete Beach, Florida

It goes without saying that you should never have more children than you have car windows.

—Erma Bombeck, married to Bill from
1949 until her death in 1996.

❧

Please Don't Eat the Daisies
BY JEAN KERR

We are being very careful with our children. They'll never have to pay a psychiatrist to find out why we rejected them. We'll tell them why we rejected them. Because they're impossible, that's why.

It seems to me, looking back on it, that everything was all right when there were two of them and two of us. We felt loved, protected, secure. But now that there are four of them and two of us, things have changed. We're in the minority, we're not as vigorous as we used to be and it's clear that we cannot compete with these younger men.

You take Christopher—and you *may;* he's a slightly used eight-year-old. The source of our difficulty with him lies in the fact that he is interested in the precise values of words whereas we are only interested in having him pick his clothes up off the floor. I say, "Christopher, you take a bath and put all your things in the wash," and he says, "Okay, but it will break the Bendix." Now at this point the shrewd rejoinder would be, "That's all right, let it break the Bendix." But years of experience have washed over me in vain and I, perennial patsy, inquire, "*Why* will it break the wash?" So he explains, "Well, if I put *all* my things in the wash, I'll have to put my shoes in and they will certainly break the machinery."

"Very well," I say, all sweetness and control, "put everything but the shoes in the wash." He picks up my agreeable tone at once, announcing cheerily, "Then you *do* want me to put my belt in the wash." I don't know what I say at this point, but my husband says, "*Honey*, you mustn't scream at him that way."

Another version of this battle of semantics would be:

"Don't kick the table leg with your foot."

"I'm not kicking, I'm tapping."

"Well, don't tap with your foot."

"It's not my foot, it's a fork."

"Well don't tap with the fork."

"It's not a *good* fork." . . . et cetera, et cetera.

Christopher is an unusual child in other respects. I watch him from the kitchen window. With a garden rake in one hand he scampers up a tree, out across a long branch, and down over the stone wall—as graceful and as deft as a squirrel. On the other hand, he is unable to get from the living room into the front hall without bumping into at least two pieces of furniture. (I've seen him hit as many as five, but that's championship stuff and he can't do it every time.)

He has another trick, which defies analysis, and also the laws of gravity. He can walk out into the middle of a perfectly empty kitchen and trip on the linoleum. I *guess* it's the linoleum. There isn't anything else there.

My friends who have children are always reporting the quaint and agreeable utterances of their little ones. For example, the mother of one five-year-old philosopher told me that when she appeared at breakfast in a new six-dollar pink wrap-around, her little boy chirped, in a tone giddy with wonder, "Oh, look our Miss Mommy must be going to a wedding!" Now I don't think any one of my children would say a thing like that. (What do I mean I don't *think*; there are some things about which you can be positive.) Of course, in a six-dollar wraparound I wouldn't look as if I were going to a wedding. I'd look as if I were going to paint the garage. But that's not the point. The point is: where is that babbling, idiotic loyalty that other mothers get?

A while back I spoke of a time when there were two of them and two of us. In my affinity for round numbers I'm falsifying the whole picture. Actually, there never were two of them. There was one of them, and all of a sudden there were three of them.

The twins are four now, and for several years we have had galvanized iron fencing lashed onto the outside of their bedroom windows. This gives the front of the house a rather institutional look and contributes to unnecessary rumors about my mental health, but it does keep them off the roof, which is what we had in mind.

For twins they are very dissimilar. Colin is tall and active and Johnny is short and middle-aged. Johnny doesn't kick off his shoes, he doesn't swallow beer caps or tear pages out of the telephone book. I don't think he ever draws pictures with my best lipstick. In fact, he has none of the charming, lighthearted "boy" qualities that precipitate so many scenes of violence in the home. On the other hand, he has a feeling for order and a passion for system that would be trying in a head nurse. If his pajamas are hung on the third hook in the closet instead of on the second hook, it causes him real pain. If one slat in a Venetian blind is tripped in the wrong direction he can't have a moment's peace until somebody fixes it. Indeed, if one of the beans on his plate is slightly longer than the others he can scarcely bear to eat it. It's hard for him to live with the rest of us. And vice versa.

Colin is completely different. He has a lightness of touch and a dexterity that will certainly put him on top of the heap if he ever takes up safe-cracking. Equipped with only a spoon and an old emery board, he can take a door off its hinges in seven minutes and remove all of the towel racks from the bathroom in five.

Gilbert is only seventeen months old, and it's too early to tell about him. (As a matter of fact, we can tell, all right; but we're just not ready to face it.) Once upon a time we might have been taken in by smiles and gurgles and round blue eyes, but no more. We know he is just biding his time. Today he can't do much more than eat his shoelaces and suck off an occasional button. Tomorrow, the world.

My real problem with children is that I haven't any imagination. I'm always warning them against the commonplace defections while they are planning the bizarre and unusual. Christopher gets up ahead of the rest of us on Sunday mornings and he has long since been given a list of clear directives: "Don't wake the baby," "Don't go outside in your pajamas," "Don't eat cookies before breakfast." But I never told him, "Don't make flour paste and glue together all the pages of the magazine section of the Sunday *Times*." Now I tell him, of course.

And then last week I had a dinner party and told the twins and Christopher not to go in the living room, not to use the guest towels in the bathroom, and not to leave the bicycles on the front steps. However, I neglected to tell them not to eat the daisies on the dining-room table. This was a serious omission, as I discovered when I came upon my centerpiece—a charming three-point arrangement of green stems.

The thing is, I'm going to a psychiatrist and find out why I have this feeling of persecution . . . this sense of being continually surrounded. . . .

Jean Kerr is an author and playwright whose best-selling book *Please Don't Eat the Daisies* became a popular movie and a television series.

⁂

The value of marriage is not that adults produce children, but that children produce adults.
—Peter DeVries

My husband made it clear before we married that he was not interested in having children. I needed to decide whether I could live with that decision. I took plenty of time to think about our future with and without kids. I spent a lot of time with my friends' kids and my nephew and nieces, with the idea that I might never have these young minds and hearts and souls to nurture and grow into healthy, happy adults. After taking my time and considering all the possibilities I realized that I did not need to have children of my own. It became apparent in those months of consideration that in fact I could have precious moments with children, but they would just be other people's children. I could still nurture and advise and love all the children I chose to. Once the decision was made it has been an easy one to live with. We have plenty of family on both sides to surround ourselves with whenever we like. We have other people's children come visit without their parents, giving the parents and kids a break from one another and allowing us to enjoy time with children without the full commitment. In the end it was the correct decision for us and we are happy with the choice we have made. The key is to realize there are a lot of different ways to consider having children or not.

—Marge Cole
Annapolis, Maryland

꙰

Our New Son

BY ROY ROGERS

While we were in New York performing at the rodeo in the days after little Robin passed away we got the call we had been waiting for from Miss Carson, the matron at Hope Cottage. She said that Mary Doe was ours to adopt if we wanted her. We arranged to pick her up on our way home to California. That was just grand, and Dale and I were tickled to death, but I got to thinking that one more little girl—"Dodie" we started to call her even before we picked her up—would bring the total of females in the Rogers house to four. Dusty and I were the only boys around . . . I felt pretty strong about wanting Dusty to have a brother, and told Dale I'd like to adopt a son, too. . . .

We did a series of one-night performances before we went to Dallas to bring Dodie home. The last of them was in Cincinnati. The morning before the show, while browsing through a stack of mail, I found a note from a woman in Covington, Kentucky, just across the river from Cincinnati, who ran a private home for handicapped children. They had nineteen boys and girls there and the woman wanted to know if there would be some way to introduce one of those children—her own daughter, Penny—to Roy Rogers and Trigger if she came to the show that night. I called her and said I'd be happy to meet her and Penny. While we were talking on the phone, a notion popped into my head. "Say," I said to the woman, "you don't happen to have a little boy about five or six years old who's adoptable, do you?" I told her my boy Dusty was nearly six, and that I was looking for someone

Roy and Dale, whose home was always big enough for love.

to bring home for him, to be his brother. She said there was a boy I might like to meet. She would bring him to the show, too.

Backstage that evening, I was dressed in my full Roy Rogers getup, with hat and guns and boots. I saw the woman pushing a wheelchair with a pathetically twisted little girl with cerebral palsy in it. Beside them walked a five-year-old boy in a yellow corduroy suit and a short billed cap. He was tiny; he had blond hair and big blue eyes. I walked over to them, tipped my hat to the lady and said hello to her girl, then knelt down to the boy's level. Cautiously, I extended my hand. His eyes grew wide. He seemed timid and fearful, but he overcame his fright and boldly stuck out his hand to shake. He was weak, but I could tell he was giving that handshake everything he had. As his little hand tried to get a grip on mine, he mustered a surprisingly loud voice to say, "Howdy, pardner!"

I held the boy's hand in mine and looked at him hard. I could tell that his eyes had seen a lot of things that scared him; they looked like they held secrets too dreadful for any little boy to know. But whatever the tragedies were that brought him to the orphanage, they had not extinguished a spark of light that was still shining in him bright as Northern Lights. I picked him

up and hugged him, then put him on my shoulder and walked over to
Trigger, who was outfitted for the show, I lifted him from my shoulder and
swung him into the silver saddle on ol' Trig's back. The boy grinned ear to
ear; he just glowed. At that moment, I knew he was the one for me. He was
my son.

Roy Rogers, "King of the Cowboys," married Dale Evans, "Queen of the West,"
on New Year's Eve 1947. Roy passed away in 1998, Dale in 2001. Together they
raised nine children, natural and adopted, and were blessed with sixteen grandchildren and thirty great-grandchildren.

Becoming a dad was the best thing that ever happened to my spiritual life. I never realized how completely and fiercely I could love
another person I'd never met before.
— Tom McGrath
Chicago, Illinois

I met a wonderful woman. I knew that, hitched together, we could
sail into life. I proposed. She said yes.

The fact that she was a single mother with six children, ages 8
to 18, was just part of the pact. To outsiders, however, my taking
on six kids looked like big trouble.

Twenty-five years later I can look back, trace the six lives, their
relationships with us, and appreciate the course of their history
with me. I see the three girls at one of their weddings encircle their
mother and sing with total conviction, "You are my hero . . . you
are the wings beneath my wings." I remember all the moments
when they and their three brothers turned to us and to her for help
in times of trouble or transition, and invited us to ride with them
in their joys.

I have a sense of why those on the outside were wrong, why it
wasn't trouble at all. One, I always liked them, all six of them—
from the beginning. I felt no need to change them or to set them
straight. I just enjoyed them, pushed them only when I could ac-

cording to my best lights. Two, Sally was such a good parent. She brought all her gifts to parenting. She didn't need me to step into the trap of thinking I had to play the role of authoritarian, rule-maker, boundary enforcer. They knew from us what was right, and what was great. Three, we were blessed with our being consistently, deeply together—across the board, and they knew it.

Twenty-five years later, the gift has not only ripened, it has replicated. We now have 14 grandchildren. And, for them, I am unreservedly, blessedly, dotingly "Papa."

This last Thanksgiving all 28 members of our family—children, spouses, and grandchildren—gathered at our house. The boys brought Jim Croce and Bruce Springsteen CDs, partially, I thought, to avoid hearing Mozart all day but mainly, it turned out, so that all—babies, toddlers, preteens, and adults—could dance together and sing the words. After dinner, it evolved into a three-generation sing-a-long with solos from 3-year-olds, 5-year-olds, 7-year-olds, 30-year-olds and 50-year-olds.

Trouble? Oh no. Terrible beauty!

—Terry Rynne
Winnetka, Illinois

I've had several moments of great joy . . . but the greatest joy of them all was when my sweetheart from 6 years old on consented to become Mrs. Truman after World War I. When my daughter came that topped it.

—Harry S. Truman

I never dreamed that I was going to fall so in love with my kids, and that I was going to love my husband Michael that much more.

—Katy White
South Bend, Indiana

What amazes us is how different and yet how similar our children are. Our family is like a mosaic. Each child viewed separately gives off a unique glitter, and their special gifts seem to shine alone. When seen as a family, the children glow as one with a unified stream of colors, and their unique gifts not only reflect but enhance those of their brothers and sisters.

—Jack and Marilyn McDonnell
Arlington Heights, Illinois

I grew up in a wonderful family. I have a lot to be thankful for. And the greatest gift my parents gave to me was love. When I was a child, it never once occurred to me that the foundation upon which my security depended would ever shake.

And of all the lessons my parents taught me, the most powerful one was unspoken, the way they loved one another.

My father respected my mother as an equal, if not more. She was his best friend and, in many ways, his conscience. And I learned from them the value of a true, loving partnership that lasts for life.

They simply couldn't imagine being without each other. And for 61 years, they were by each other's side.

My parents taught me the real values in life aren't material, but spiritual. They include faith and family, duty and honor, and trying to make the world a better place.

—Al Gore, married to Tipper since 1970

My idea of heaven is to sit in the garden, read a book, play with the kids and relax. My family is the center of my life . . . I (even) like to get involved with the bonding and the changing of diapers. I figure if I change theirs today, they'll change mine in twenty or thirty years.

—Mel Gibson, married to Robyn
since 1980

Watching and supporting the growing up of Sarah, Elizabeth, and Dan—helping them fly—has been a joy for Sally and me. Being a family—sharing love and laughs—helps each of us to feel at home everywhere, and gives us strength to share our lives with others.

—John Pritscher
Evanston, Illinois

The things that stand out the most to me in my life are the small things like seeing my first child smile at me. Seeing him take his first step, or the friendship that I've developed between myself and my children. These things stand out more, they mean more to me, than the actual activity on the football field.

Please, spend time with your kids. Make sure they are very important to you. Make sure that they are your focus, because if your children and your family are in focus, then when you come to the workplace, you'll be a much happier person and you're going to be a much easier person to get things accomplished with. It's amazing.

It's sort of like a booster shot when you spend time with your kids. They can turn you on to some things that you never knew. All I ask of people I talk to and meet is that they spend at least thirty minutes—just start out with thirty minutes a day—and sit down one-on-one talking to your children. Find out what they're doing, what their life is all about, what their problems are and what they feel is important to them. It's the best medicine you can have, better than chicken soup.

Make sure your children know how important they are to you, because you never know when you won't get a chance to say it. Always do that, so they know.

> —Walter Payton (all-time NFL rushing
> champion and role model who passed
> away in 1999 at age 45)

Success would be meaningless without anyone to share it with. Family will be there after everything's gone and I'm too old or tired to do this anymore.

> —Faith Hill, married to Tim McGraw
> since 1996

Marriage is special because it is our only opportunity to choose a member of our family—our spouse. All other members are chosen for us by fate.

> —Bonnie Butera
> Cos Cob, Connecticut

At this stage of life, with the children grown and gone, think how sad it would be not to have each other. We're still able to look at each other in the morning and say, "Gee, I'm glad you're here."

—Cokie Roberts, married to
Steve Roberts since 1966

"How do you like living in an Empty Nest?" an acquaintance asked as we stood next to each other in a buffet line at a potluck dinner.

I've gotten that question often this year, probably because many people know that I used to dread the thought of living in an Empty Nest. But now that my husband Lynn and I have reached the end of our first year in this new season of life, I have a different perspective.

"The Empty Nest is a bad name for a good place," I told her as we spooned our way through a variety of salads.

She looked a bit surprised, so I started to explain just as we reached the chicken casseroles and lasagnas. "The Empty Nest sounds like a bad place because the word *empty* implies there is nothing left in a home after the children move out. It sounds like a place where the parents wander aimlessly through quiet rooms, mourning their *full* pasts and *empty* futures.

"Now I do admit that after we took Kendall, our youngest, off to college, I faced a period of transition when I grieved the passing of a precious era. But slowly, Lynn and I began to discover the good parts of this simpler new chapter of life."

"Like what?" she asked.

"Like the freedom to eat only baked potatoes for dinner at eight. Or work all afternoon on a project without worrying about taking care of others. Or, best of all, the joy of rekindling our relationship, often neglected by the demanding distractions of children. In the last year we've gone on more bike rides and walks, rented more movies, and spent more time sharing our thoughts with each other. We've grown to depend on each other in a whole new way.

"The empty nest is full of potential," I concluded, just as we reached the yummy desserts . . . which seemed entirely appropriate.

—Carol Kuykendall
Boulder, Colorado

The heart that loves is always young.
—Greek proverb

Poinsettias in December

BY OSSIE DAVIS

Dear Ruby,

Every December the ninth, you and I go out and buy the biggest, most beautiful poinsettia we can find. Christmas, New Year's, Mother's Day, Father's Day, your birthday or mine, none of these will matter after that; no other presents, no cards, no furs, no smoking jackets, no diamonds, and no yachts—only this one, solitary commemoration of our wedding anniversary. That is the only gift we give each other during the year. Not only does that save us from the hype and hoopla that have swallowed up the meaning of our holidays, but also we know that the only true gift is yourself—your undivided attention, for richer, for poorer, in sickness and in health, till death us do part—and time on the cross together, and listening, and silences together, and wishing the best for each other . . . and willingness to learn and stand corrected. . . .

I look back now, in praise and deep thanksgiving to you, Ruby, the woman I love, seeing not two of us, but one—not certain where I end and you begin. One thing is certain: The best of me has been subsidized by the best of what you are. I have no hungers that you do not feed. And only this poinsettia—the biggest, prettiest, most expensive in the house—can say that for me.

Chapter Eleven

HAPPY ANNIVERSARY!

To grow old
is a glorious thing
when one has not
unlearned
what it means
to begin.
— Martin Buber

Grow old along with me!
The best is yet to be,
The last of life, for which the first was made:
Our times are in his hand
Who saith, "A whole I planned,
Youth shows but half; trust God: see all, nor be afraid!"
                                        —Robert Browning

❦

The Promised Land

BY BILL COSBY

Grow old along with me!
The best is yet to be.

When Browning wrote these lines, he wasn't thinking of my mother and father or anyone else in North Philadelphia; but whenever I see my mother and father together, I know they're residing in a state where I want to live with Camille, a state of such blessed mellowness that they make the Dalai Lama seem like a Type A personality.

I will never forget my first awareness that my mother and father had ascended to a matrimonial plane where only God knew what they were doing—perhaps. We were driving to Philadelphia from Atlantic City, with my father at the wheel, my mother beside him, and me in the back.

"Oh, there's a car from Pittsburgh," said my mother, looking at a license plate in the next lane. "How do you know it's from Pittsburgh?" said my father.

"Because I couldn't think of Pennsylvania," she replied.

And I waited for my father to respond to this Einsteinian leap into another dimension, but he didn't speak. He simply continued to drive, a supremely contented man.

Because he had understood.

He had understood that my mother's Pittsburgh was a mythical place, located where the Monongahela entered the twilight zone. My mother also had not been able to think of Afghanistan, but she didn't say that the car was from Kabul. However, *had* she said that the car was from Kabul, my father would have understood it bore Afghans moving to Allentown.

For the next twenty minutes, I thought about fifty-three years of marriage and how they had bonded my parents in this remarkable Zen rapport; but then I was suddenly aware that my father had just driven past the exit for Philadelphia. Not the exit for Pennsylvania or for North America, but for Philadelphia, the literal city.

"Mom," I said, "didn't Dad just pass the exit we want?"

"Yes, he did," she replied.

"Well, why don't you *say* something?"

"Your father knows what he's doing."

Had *I* driven past the proper exit, my wife would have said, *Please pull over and let me out. I'd like to finish this trip by hitching a ride on a chicken truck.*

But if Camille and I can just stay together another twenty-five years, then we also will have reached the Twilight Zone, where one of us will do something idiotic and the other one not only will understand it but admire it as well.

You turned out the light where I'm reading, I will tell her. *Thank you for the surprise trip to the planetarium.*

You left your shoes in the bathtub, she will tell me. *Thank you for giving me two more boats.*

One morning a few days after that memorably roundabout trip to Philadelphia, I got another glimpse of the lotus land where my parents dwelled. My father came into the house, took off his hat, put it on a chair, gave some money to my children, and then went back and sat on his hat.

"You just sat on your hat," my mother told him.

"Of course I did," he replied, and then neither one of them said another word about hat reduction. When the time came to leave, my father picked up the crushed hat and put it on his head, where it sat like a piece of Pop Art. My mother glanced at it, as if to make sure that it would not fall off, and then she took his arm and they walked out the door, ready to be the sweethearts of the Mummers Parade.

However, if *I* sat on my hat, Camille would say, *Can't you feel that you're sitting on your hat?*

And I would reply, *It's a tradition in my family for a man to sit on his hat. It's one of the little things that my father did for my mother.*

Yes, twenty-five years, happy as they have been, are still not enough to have given Camille and me that Ringling Brothers rhythm my mother and father enjoy. But we can hear the circus calling to us.

Love, what follies are committed in thy name, said Francis Bacon.

So far, most of marriage has been the Ziegfeld Follies for Camille and me. And now we're getting ready to send in the clowns.

Bill Cosby, comedian and author of *Love and Marriage,* has been married to Camille since 1964.

Thursday will be thirty-two years. What a thirty-two years! I've never been anything but happy for that anniversary. Maybe I haven't given you all you're entitled to, but I've done my best, and I'm still in love with the prettiest girl in the world.

—Harry S. Truman

Dear Barbara,

Will you marry me? Oops, I forgot, you did that 49 years ago today! I was very happy on that day in 1945, but I am even happier today. You have given me joy that few men know. You have made our boys into men by bawling them out and then, right away, by loving them. You have helped Doro be the sweetest greatest daughter in the whole wide world. I have climbed perhaps the highest mountain in the world, but even that cannot hold a candle to being Barbara's husband. Mum used to tell me: "Now, George, don't walk ahead." Little did she know I was only trying to keep up—keep up with Barbara Pierce from Onondaga Street in Rye, New York. I love you!

—George Bush

Harold and I have been together now for almost forty years. To me he hasn't changed much from the slender, exuberant youth ice-skating across the Boston Common. To me he is still the young man who held my hand as we waded along the edge of the waves of Lime Tree Beach in St. Thomas. The night was warm, the breeze was soft, and the ocean glimmered with phosphorescent creatures. Harold had just accepted the commissioner's job and was bursting with excitement and ideas. "Can it ever get better than this?" we wondered that night. It did.

—Shirlee Taylor Haizlip
Los Angeles, California

The following comments were taken down at a New Year's Eve party in Greenwich, Connecticut on the eve of the new millennium, 2001.

I like being married because it's an easy date. Mark and I have been married 27 years now, and he's still the best date anybody could ever have.

—Peggy Geimer
Greenwich, Connecticut

I always told him: if someone better comes along, you're out the door. Well, it's 55 years later, and Bob's still here. No one has ever come close.

—Jill Curran
Palm City, Florida

We've been clowning around together for 32 years. We met over coffee and doughnuts at medical school. She asked me why I wanted to be a doctor. I told her because I wanted to be rich and play God.

And I told him, "You're just what I'm looking for." We both became rich in love and are still having fun.

—Joe and Mary Watts
Greenwich, Connecticut

Sixty years ago when I first met Nancy, I told my best friend, "Now there's an interesting gal! I'd like to get to know her better." Believe it or not, I got to know her better and it turns out she's the most interesting person I've ever known.

George told me this story six months ago and I was amazed. Because I said the same thing about him to my girlfriend! I got to know him better, too, and to this day no one is more interesting to me than George.

—George and Nancy Chelwick
Greenwich, Connecticut

Ten, nine, eight, seven . . . *Happy New Year!*
—Everybody

Ken and I were married on June 27, 1968. Next month will be our thirty-third anniversary. We were quite young when we met in 1967—I was a 19-year-old college student and he was 22 and in graduate school. Ken and I met in my junior year and got married a month after my graduation. I thought he was funny, handsome, and trustworthy, but we didn't really know each other all that well.

Why are we still together and still happy about it? It's not simply inertia and the security of knowing who you're going to go out with on New Year's Eve, though that's part of it. If you're in it for the long haul, you have to expect that you and your partner are going to grow and change a lot. We weathered the cataclysmic social movements of the '70s and '80s, and each allowed the other to change. I became a feminist, Ken had to start doing dishes (he joked that every time I came back from a consciousness-raising meeting, he had more to do). He wanted to travel, so we quit our jobs and went to South America for six months. We took turns supporting each other through job and career changes. We called each other's parents "Mom" and "Dad." We took classes together— TM, yoga, tennis, photography, and other stuff we don't do anymore. We tried different religions (I was a Christian Scientist, he was Jewish) and ended up compromising as Unitarians.

After seven years we became parents ourselves—the most challenging part of the whole deal. Ken turned out to be a wonderful, calm father, which deepened my love for him. I was more hysterical, but he stood by me. Our personalities were complementary— I was more emotional, he was more rational. But we have learned from each other and are probably rather similar now. Through deaths of parents, a bout with cancer, two corneal transplants, countless parenthood triumphs and tragedies, and just plain old boring everyday life, we have held hands. Each of us thinks we are the luckier of the two. Each of us wants the other's highest good. We still laugh a lot, and we still hold hands.

—Wendy Schuman
Montclair, New Jersey

∽

As Time Goes By

BY TOM MCGRATH

June 26, 1962, was the most significant date of my young life. That was the day we celebrated my grandparents' 50th wedding anniversary. I was 13 years old and it was a day full of lessons I'll never forget.

Consider this: in 1908, a young man and a young woman, still in their teens and unknown to each other, leave their troubled homeland, board a ship for a perilous voyage, arrive in a strange city in a new country, meet, and fall in love. They find work, get married, establish a household, make new friends, start a family, join a parish, help others come over from Ireland, make more friends, learn new ways, hang on to some of the old ways, raise their kids, celebrate their joys, and mourn their losses. In the whisk of a minute, 50 years go by.

In the grand scheme of events transpiring in the 20th century, the married life of these two people don't amount to a hill of beans, to quote Humphrey Bogart in *Casablanca*. And yet . . .

I was an altar boy that day at the Mass celebrating their 50 years of life together. And as I looked out at the packed pews of Visitation Church that morning, I got a sense of the profound effect that can flow from saying "I do" and meaning it. Because of these two people, Thomas and Margaret McGrath, a streetcar conductor and a homemaker, hundreds had gathered to pray and pay tribute to them and also to honor the glory of life itself. In the congregation were neighbors, friends, and relatives (shirttail and otherwise). At Mass, and later at the raucous reception, the crowd was dotted with a few bigwigs and *monsignori,* but mostly filled with first- and second-generation immigrants inching their way to respectability. These were hard-working people who came to celebrate many small miracles: the daily application of intentions declared 50 years before. We ate and drank and told stories. We sang the old songs and the new and oh, how we danced.

And what did this 13-year-old boy think of all this? I know I couldn't have put it into words at the time, but the lessons were emblazoned on my heart: that choices do matter. That fidelity counts. That I belonged to a story that was bigger and grander than I had ever realized or could imagine.

I saw that the life of two people, my grandparents, had added to the quality and goodness of the life of hundreds, possibly thousands of others. I saw the theology of marriage written plain that day.

Celebrating a wedding anniversary, like love, is a many-splendored thing. It's a public proclamation of the grace of the sacrament, an invitation to gain spiritual strength from the life of commitment that brings forth new life. It's a sign to all that can build up the community. It can also provide a spiritual boost to the celebrating couple. I found that to be so on my own 10th anniversary.

A decade into our marriage, Kathleen and I were different people from the naïve pups we'd been on our wedding day. We knew more about each other, about ourselves, and about the demands life can make on you. We were at a crossroads, and our marriage could have gone either way: growth and new commitment or stagnation and, at a minimum, spiritual divorce. After an eye-opening marriage encounter, we knew a party was in order. We gathered family and friends and fellow parishioners for a 10th anniversary Mass and celebration in our home. It was a great time and in many ways I count that as the day I truly said, "I do."

Taking stock on significant anniversaries is a great way to strengthen your commitment and to celebrate the life you continue to choose, day by day, over time. And it's a wonderful way to witness the power of God in your life over time. As I write this, my siblings and I are planning my parents' 50th wedding-anniversary celebration. Life goes on. The story continues to unfold. The two people who first revealed the face of God to me will face each other again and say, "I do."

I'm glad that my daughters will witness that and be part of the crowd of people their grandparents have laughed with, cried with, confided in, relied on, and loved well. And that seems something worth celebrating.

Tom McGrath is the Family Life editor for *U.S. Catholic* magazine and has been married to Kathleen since 1976.

❦

I recently attended my parents' fiftieth wedding anniversary. I'd had it in my mind to ask each of them, privately, whether, knowing what they do now, they'd do it all over again. But I didn't ask them. Because on the day of the party, my father showed me what he'd given my mother for a gift. She was wearing a gold necklace with a capital L encrusted with diamonds.

"That L stands for 50," my father said. "I didn't know if you knew."

"Actually," I said, "I thought it stood for love."

"Well," he said. "That, too."

"And what did you get for a present?" I asked my father. At the very same moment that I heard my mother answer, "A kaleidoscope," I heard my father say, "Why, the great pleasure of seeing her wear the necklace, of course."

Pretty romantic words from a man who rarely says much. But even clearer than what he said was the way my parents looked at each other, what was in their faces. I knew that if I asked them, they would each say they'd do it again. Because there is something to the silent testimony of the simple passage of time. There is something to a large group of people gathering to congratulate you on being together so long, and the two of you smiling, nodding, and saying nothing more than "Thank you."

—Elizabeth Berg

When we go to weddings, at least ones where the couple recites traditional vows, we find ourselves becoming awfully sentimental and teary. I've noticed that's true of other long-married couples, who nod their way through the ceremony, squeezing each other's hand as the bride and groom pledge "to have and to hold, from this day forward." Those newlyweds can't possibly know what that promise will mean. We didn't either, when we said those words under the *chuppah* that beautiful September night when we were so young. We've been incredibly blessed. So far, we've lived for better, not worse, richer, not poorer, in health, not sickness. Still, after thirty-three years, we can't anticipate what will happen from this day forward. But we're eager to find out.

—Cokie Roberts, married to Steve
since 1966

On our wedding anniversary last year my husband presented me with a small package wrapped in beautiful silver papers. It was about the right size for a bracelet.

I tossed Sandy a smile and opened the box. Inside was a metal chain, composed of three links. Not three links of delicate gold chain, mind you, but the kind of heavy chain you use to fasten the gate on a fence.

I could think of nothing to say. Somehow, "Thank you for this portion of chain link fence" didn't seem appropriate. Sandy reached over and lifted the three links from the box. "Do you notice how the two links on each end are joined by the center link?" he said. "They are separate and complete in themselves, yet they share a common space together. I think it is a picture of marriage at its best—two people, complete and independent in themselves, but joined in a common bond of intimacy."

As I took the chain in my hands, I felt a slight stinging in my eyes. Even the bracelet I received from him later did not affect me so deeply as that strong and tender symbol of what a relationship can be. Whether husband and wife, parent and child, or simply close friends, the link needs the balance of autonomy and intimacy in order to remain strong.

—Sue Monk Kidd
Mt. Pleasant, South Carolina

Can You Top This?
BY JOHN D. LEINBACH

Marriage is not as popular as it used to be, but it's still worth the price of admission. Take my own case. Years ago—fifty-five, if you need to know—it came my turn. Take my word: I never knew what true happiness was until I got married. Then it was too late.

Let's be serious. Most people you know consider themselves lucky to be married, and especially lucky to have the mate they have. (If my wife contradicts this statement, don't pay attention. She just likes to talk.)

To put it plainly, the only thing better than a good marriage is ice cream for breakfast.

Just mull the alternative. Take all those fun things you could do when you were single. Blind dates; you had to be blind to enjoy them. Parties and dances? Remember the time your date disap-

John loves Mary in 1946.

peared with your best friend? And those morning-after hangovers when you couldn't even remember whether or not you'd had a good time, and weren't even sure of your name—which you might have recalled if only that damned dog of your neighbor's would stop barking?

You call that fun?

Now contrast that with the rewarding serenity of married life. A quiet evening at home, just you and your mate, giving each other the silent treatment. Who cares about the neighbor's barking dog? Hey, you can't even hear that hound over the racket your kids are making. Admit it—pure bliss. How do you top that?

More to the point, how do you reach this state of marital bliss? How does it all start?

First you have to fall in love. Easy enough, you say. Some people fall in love once a week. With a different dreamboat. A few even fall in love with the neighbor's barking dog. There is no help for them.

But you've got to be choosy; it's a big commitment. So you'll want to pick someone who has interests similar to your own, someone you can carry on a conversation with. You can't spend every night glued to the TV or computer. Take a man I know who has been married and divorced four times. Not good marriage material, you say? Don't be so sure. Recently he married a woman who had been divorced *five* times. The two are as happy as clams. (Incidentally, clams are happiest when they're not being eaten.) Mainly, this pair is happy because they have a topic they can hash and rehash: their former partners! Now I don't recommend that to you. But it's one way.

Another thing. Don't shy away from arguing. You can't talk about the weather all the time. Or what the kids did today—which might easily start an argument, anyway. So argue away. About what? Whatever comes to mind. With skill, you can keep it going to exhaustion. And then get a good night's sleep.

Of course, in every marriage, someone has to be the boss. The husband invariably believes he's it. Only later does he begin to suspect that somebody else in the family is in charge. Let me be personal. I was aware of this trap. So, before our marriage I made an agreement with my intended: I would make the big decisions and she would make the small ones. Well, we've been married fifty-five years now and no big decisions have come up! It's a no-win situation. Still, I keep hoping.

But then, if you're already married, you know all these peculiarities. And you're too happy to care about them anyway. Where else would you find someone who thinks you're the greatest? Who cares for you in sickness, and in haste so as not to be late at the golf course? Who defends you even from your mother-in-law, if somewhat halfheartedly? Who is able to analyze the bad traits in your kids and attribute all of them to your family? Who sympathizes with you when you suffer reversals? Who rejoices with you when you do well, then boasts about you to the neighbors? I ask you: Who else?

One caution: As the years go by, a gnawing fear creeps into each spouse's mind. What if I should lose my mate? What if my spouse should die? What then?

The horrible conclusion: You'd be all alone. Back to blind dates, parties and dances as a solo, and barking dogs.

Not a pretty picture, is it? So enjoy

Half a century later nothing that is real has changed.

your marital blessings while you can. And be sure to tell your spouse you don't know why you've put up with all those pranks all these years.

Then smile, because you know you wouldn't change anything.

John Leinbach started his career writing jokes for Bing Crosby, Don Ameche, and other radio stars. Later he became creative director for BBD&O advertising agency. He has been married to Mary since 1946.

⌒∞०

Those who love deeply never grow old; they may die of old age, but they die young.

—Sir Arthur Wing Pinero

When you are old and gray and full of sleep,
And nodding by the fire, take down this book,
And slowly read, and dream of the soft look
Your eyes had once, and of their shadows deep;

How many loved your moments of glad grace,
And loved your beauty with love false or true;
But one man loved the pilgrim soul in you,
And loved the sorrows of your changing face.

—William Butler Yeats

We've been married one week, and have discovered how much farther our arms can wrap around the other.

—Mary Beth and Mark Redmond
Yonkers, New York

We've been married one day, and we cannot believe we get to live with each other's best friend for the rest of our lives.

—Jeremy and Elizabeth Langford
Evanston, Illinois

Tribute to Sergei

BY EKATERINA GORDEEVA

Olympic pair skaters Ekaterina Gordeeva and Sergei Grinkov celebrated their love on and off the ice until Sergei's tragic death in 1995. Katia writes the following piece about the first time she skated alone . . . in his memory.

As the time neared for my solo number, I thought about the words Sergei used to say to me when we were getting ready to skate. We always kissed each other before we skated, we always hugged and touched each other. Now, in the tunnel, waiting to go on the ice, I didn't have anyone to touch or kiss. It was a terrible feeling to be standing there by myself. Only Dave, the production manager for Stars on Ice, was there watching, and I could tell he was thinking the same thing: How sad to see her standing here without Sergei.

But as soon as the Mahler music started to play, and I skated out into the darkened arena, the bad feelings went away. The lights rose, the people started to applaud, and I had a feeling I'd never experienced before. I'd been worried that I'd be lost out there by myself, that I'd be so small no one would see me. But I felt so much bigger than I am. I felt huge, suddenly, like I filled the entire ice.

As the people clapped at the beginning of the program, I wondered whether I should stop. I wanted to thank them for coming from all over the country, all over the world, to think of Sergei. But my legs kept moving. I thought, I can't stop or I'll lose all this magic and power. I just listened to my legs. And I listened to Sergei. It was like I had double power. I never felt so much power in myself, so much energy. I'd start a movement, and someone would finish it for me. I didn't have a thing in my head. It was all in my heart, all in my soul.

Chapter Twelve

LOVE IS STRONGER THAN DEATH

They whom we love
and lose
are no longer
where they were before.
They are now
wherever we are.
St. John Chrysostom

When I met Alfred my self-esteem was no higher than a bird with one wing. In our 28 years together I learned to love myself as he loved me. It is what he gave me that enabled me to get through his death and dying, and now to live a good life on my own: strength and confidence.

—Delta Willis
New Orleans, Louisiana

Like Mama and Nora, Ossie and I have also made arrangements [for our death]. Cremation after a public ceremony, and then, into the urn. A special urn, large enough and comfortable enough to hold both our ashes. Whoever goes first will wait inside for the other. When we are reunited at last, we want the family to say good-bye and seal the urn forever. Then on the side, in letters not too bold—but not too modest either—we want the following inscription:

RUBY AND OSSIE—IN THIS THING TOGETHER
    —Ruby Dee

A letter to a loved one in heaven:
Dear Andres,

Darling, I miss you so much that it became almost unbearable. I miss your kisses and hugs, your companionship.

I miss your getting up before me to wash up and prepare breakfast while I made the bed and took a bath. I loved to sit down to a good breakfast, to be waited on while we chatted with each other.

In the evening when we both came home from work, you either prepared supper or you'd take me to a cafeteria. How much I appreciated that!

I loved to see you, after supper, relax in your comfortable easy chair when you watched TV. Often you fell asleep and snored. Even that I miss!

When you got up from your chair, you went outside to check all the locks to make sure everything was safe and secure. While you did that I walked back and forth along the long driveway for my exercise.

When we came inside, I prepared a mug of hot chocolate for you to drink before we went to bed.

As we lay in bed, you were such a comfort. I felt so safe and secure. The touch of your skin was so soft, smooth and lean that I called you My Lean Rabbit. I loved all of that and miss it more than you know.

The first few weeks after you left me for heaven were terribly upsetting and full of tears. One morning when I stopped the car to open the gate, the car started rolling toward me and on to the end of the driveway, out on the street and up the incline of the vacant lots across the street. Sheer panic! As the car climbed up the curb, it rolled back to the street and into the driveway where I was able to stop it. I thought of injury to myself, damage to the car and other vehicles, and people who could be driving or walking by. Fortunately, no cars drove by and no people walked by while the car was uncontrollable. What a scare! And afterwards what a relief. Were you and God watching out for me?

I'm looking forward to the time when we'll be together again. I'm sure there is a space for me in your mansion. There we'll live happily forever and ever!

Your loving wife,
Ana [Arcadia Lopez]
San Antonio, Texas

Do not stand at my grave and weep;
I am not there. I do not sleep.
I am a thousand winds that blow;
I am the diamond glints on snow.
I am the sunlight on ripened grain;
I am the gentle autumn rain.
When you awaken in the morning hush,
I am the swift uplifting rush
Of quiet birds in circled flight.
I am the soft star that shines at night.
Do not stand at my grave and cry.
I am not there; I did not die.

—Author unknown

c∞ɔ

Too Perfect to Last

BY C. S. LEWIS

"It was too perfect to last," so I am tempted to say of our marriage. But it can be meant in two ways. It may be grimly pessimistic—as if God no sooner saw two of His creatures happy than He stopped it ("None of that here!"). As if He were like the Hostess at the sherry-party who separates two guests the moment they show signs of having got into a real conversation. But it could also mean "This had reached its proper perfection. This had become what it had in it to be. Therefore of course it would not be prolonged." As if God said, "Good; you have mastered that exercise. I am very pleased with it. And now you are ready to go on to the next." When you have learned to do quadratics and enjoy doing them you will not be set them much longer. The teacher moves you on.

For we did learn and achieve something. There is, hidden or flaunted, a sword between the sexes till an entire marriage reconciles them. It is arrogance in us to call frankness, fairness, and chivalry "masculine" when we see them in a woman; it is arrogance in them, to describe a man's sensitiveness or tact or tenderness as "feminine." But also what poor, warped fragments of humanity most mere men and mere women must be to make the implications of that arrogance plausible. Marriage heals this. Jointly the two become fully human. "In the image of God He created *them*." Thus, by a paradox, this carnival of sexuality leads us out beyond our sexes.

And then one or other dies. And we think of this as love cut short; like a dance stopped in mid career or a flower with its head unluckily snapped off—something truncated and therefore, lacking its due shape. I wonder. If, as I can't help suspecting, the dead also feel the pains of separation (and this may be one of their purgatorial sufferings), then for both lovers, and for all pairs of lovers without exception, bereavement is a universal and integral part of our experience of love. It follows marriage as normally as marriage follows courtship or as autumn follows summer. It is not a truncation of the process but one of its phases; not the interruption of the dance, but the next figure. We are "taken out of ourselves" by the loved one while she is here. Then comes the tragic figure of the dance in which we must learn to be still taken out of ourselves though the bodily presence is withdrawn, to love the very Her, and not fall back to loving our past, or our memory, or our sorrow, or our relief from sorrow, or our own love. . . .

What we want is to live our marriage well and faithfully through that phase too. If it hurts (and it certainly will) we accept the pains as a necessary part of this phase. We don't want to escape them at the price of desertion or divorce. Killing the dead a second time. We were one flesh. Now that it has been cut in two, we don't want to pretend that it is whole and complete. We will be still married, still in love. Therefore we shall still ache. But we are not at all—if we understand ourselves—seeking the aches for their own sake. The less of them the better, so long as the marriage is preserved. And the more joy there can be in the marriage between dead and living, the better.

C. S. Lewis, best-selling author and theologian, was married to Joy Gresham from 1956 until her death in 1960.

⌒∞⌒

I knelt and prayed by the beloved shrine. Yet thank God! I feel more and more that my beloved one is *everywhere* not only there!
—Queen Victoria

Love will never die. Once you know somebody, you can never un-know that person. And knowing is loving. So you can never get out of love. There might be misunderstandings and separating for other reasons, but love is always there. . . . Love is a soul thing. It stays there.

—Yoko Ono, married to John Lennon
from 1969 until his death in 1980

So many uncanny events marked the period of time following Michael's death that I really learned not to question or analyze them, but rather to simply receive them as precious gifts. The entire period of his illness and the year that followed were marked by what felt like showers of holy water—incredible coincidences and stunning series of events unfolding in such ways as to be powerful messages. What I have learned with complete conviction is that the death of my husband was not the end of our relationship. As I honored my own process of grief and I listened with my heart I began to really experience his presence in my life.

—Cindy Lou Rowe

[My friend] Carol's husband was killed in an accident last year. Jim, only fifty-two, was driving home from work. The other driver was a teenager with a very high blood-alcohol level. Jim died instantly. The teenager was in the emergency room less than two hours.

There were other ironic twists: It was Carol's fiftieth birthday, and Jim had two plane tickets to Hawaii in his pocket. He was going to surprise her. Instead, he was killed by a drunken driver.

"How have you survived this?" I finally asked Carol a year later.

Her eyes welled up with tears. I thought I had said the wrong thing, but she gently took my hand and said, "It's all right, Debbi. I want to tell you. . . . The day I married him, I promised I would never let him leave the house in the morning without telling him I loved him. He made the same promise. It got to be a joke between us, and as babies came along, it got to be a hard promise to keep. I remember running down the driveway, saying 'I love you' through clenched teeth when I was mad, driving to the office to put a note in his car. It was like a funny challenge. We made a lot of memories trying to say 'I love you' before noon every day of our married life.

"The morning Jim died, he left a birthday card in the kitchen and slipped out to the car. I heard the engine starting. *Oh, no, you don't, Buster,* I thought. I raced out and banged on the car window until he rolled it down. 'Here on my fiftieth birthday, Mr. James E. Garret. I, Carol Garret, want to go on record as saying I love you!'

"That's how I've survived, Debbi. Knowing that the last words I said to Jim were 'I love you.' "

—Debbi Smoot
Salt Lake City, Utah

꧁◈꧂

Loving Jeanne
BY PAUL SIMON

Months later we realized there had been tell-tale signs. When we played tennis Jeanne sometimes missed the ball completely as she rarely did earlier. Or not seeing a deer in our driveway when I saw it. Then one day she picked me up at my office at Southern Illinois University and as we drove to the grocery store she would have hit a parked car had I not yelled, "Watch out!" She startled me by saying, "I didn't see that car."

I thought she probably had a detached retina and we immediately made an appointment with her ophthalmologist, Dr. Michaelis Jackson. He reported the first inkling of seriously bad news. Jeanne did not have eye problems; we should consult a neurologist. We immediately made an appointment with Dr. Lori Hopkins, who instructed Jeanne to have an MRI, a form of X ray. Then Dr. Hopkins delivered the bad news: a brain tumor, probably malignant. Jeanne needed surgery. Dr. Hopkins told us it could be performed in a local hospital. I asked where she would go if her husband had a brain tumor. "Houston," she replied. "That's where we're going," I told her.

When we walked out of her office, Jeanne cried a little. At that point I didn't. "We're going to lick this thing," I had already told myself in the physician's office. That determination, plus some anger at whatever forces permitted this to happen to Jeanne, kept me going.

At Houston—which has the largest medical center in the world with 7,500 employees—we met with Dr. David S. Baskin. He explained what Jeanne would be experiencing, that she should stay for a few days after the surgery in the hotel adjoining in the hospital. He did not paint a rosy picture but not a gloomy one. By that time we had learned there are different types of brain cancer, and he outlined what each might mean.

Shortly after we arrived our son, Martin, who lives with his family in a Washington, D.C., suburb, joined us. And our daughter, Sheila, from our home area of Carbondale, Illinois, left her family to join us.

The operation took five hours, and that evening Dr. Baskin met with us and told us that she had gliosarcoma, the second most deadly form of brain cancer. Ordinarily a person lives about six months after its discovery, he said, but each individual is different and Jeanne might die sooner, or might live much longer.

Less than a day after the operation she walked on her own. I felt optimistic.

When Jeanne returned home she led a normal life, curtailing some activities but not many. She underwent radiation treatments, wearing a mask that permitted the specialist to zero in on the precise area of the tumor. Following the radiation treatments came chemotherapy, which tired her, but it pleased both of us that she had no other side effects as many do who take chemotherapy.

Small things soon indicated deterioration. When she awoke in the morning or in the middle of the night to go to the bathroom she had to sit on the edge of the bed for a short time before she could safely walk. One night a loud crash woke me up. I jumped out of bed and found Jeanne on the floor unconscious. She had tried to walk to the bathroom. I called my daughter, Sheila, who lives ten miles away, both for immediate physical help in getting Jeanne back in bed and to join me in figuring out what to do. Having Sheila nearby was a real help, both in physically taking care of her and having someone to talk to about Jeanne's gradually worsening situation.

After her fall I put a chair and pillows on her side of our bed to remind her not to get up without getting my help.

Through all of this she maintained excellent morale. Yes, we cried together on occasion, but I tried not to do it when I was with Jeanne, to keep up her good attitude. And she maintained her optimism almost all the time. Perhaps she did it to buoy my spirits as I did for her.

Gradually, moving around became more and more difficult. I would hold her as she walked, but during the final weeks she had to use a wheelchair.

She also had more difficulty speaking, the wrong words frequently coming out though I usually could guess what she meant. All of our friends went out of their way to be helpful.

Jeanne attended church each Sunday, as she always had done. I took her to St. Francis Xavier Roman Catholic Church and walked her to her pew where Sheila and her family met her. I then went to Our Savior Lutheran Church to which I belong, a routine we had followed for years. She attended services for the last time six days before she died.

She wanted to die at home with her family around her, and she did. A few days before her death her deteriorating health took a dramatic turn for the worse. Sheila and her husband, Perry Knop, and their two daughters came to the house and Martin and his wife, Julie, and their son and daughter flew in to join us.

Jeanne was unconscious the last three days. We put her in a rented hospital bed with a slight tilt upward, facing the window, so she could see the outdoor scene that she loved in case she would regain consciousness even for a few moments. She never did.

One of the most touching things occurred when I sat with Jeanne—we alternated doing that—and our five-year-old granddaughter "CJ" totally on her own climbed up on the bed and kissed Jeanne. I still am moved to tears every time I recall that small incident. (I find as I age—I am now seventy-two—the tears flow more frequently.)

Sheila, Martin, and I planned the funeral service. Cooperating in every way, Father Robert Flannery—who had given Jeanne the anointing of the sacrament of the sick (formerly called last rites)—could not have been more helpful. Because many who would attend would not be Roman Catholic, we wanted a special memorial service rather than the traditional Catholic mass. My brother, Rev. Arthur Simon, a Lutheran minister, joined Father Flannery in officiating, as Jeanne would have wanted it. Instead of singing the hymn "Faith of Our Fathers," we changed the words to "Faith of Our Mothers."

Over a thousand people from all corners of the nation attended the visitation at the church the night before the service. People from all walks of life. People whose lives Jeanne had touched. Men I had never seen wearing ties who didn't quite know what to say, but I hope they sensed that their presence and tribute were meaningful to me. James Williams, who delivers our newspapers, not only sent flowers but sent food to our home after the funeral. All these small gestures were significant to me then and always will be.

Jeanne's positive attitude throughout her ordeal, with few complaints, will always be with me. At the memorial service for Senator Hubert Humphrey, Walter Mondale said, "He taught us how to live and how to die."

That is true of Jeanne. She contributed to libraries and literacy and the arts and went out of her way to help people. We knew when we married that ours would be lives that require sacrifice but also have rich rewards in satisfaction. We had thirty-nine great years together, good for us, but also good for others.

She would have loved the tributes paid to her after her death. And she deserved them.

For me, those first days after her death, particularly after the busyness of the visitation and memorial service, were days of unspeakable grief. Death would not have been an unwelcome visitor for me then. But slowly I focused not on the great loss, but on the good years together, and what she would have wanted me to do. That shift in attitude—and it does not come

"Service to others made our life so rich."

suddenly—makes a huge difference. Both the demands of faith and the example of her life caused that shift away from self-absorption with loss to involvement in the lives of others.

Before we married we talked about our shared hopes for life together. Neither of us had as a goal making big money. We lived comfortably, sometimes with a financial struggle requiring a bank loan, but we both knew that satisfaction in life comes from helping others. We did many things together, including political campaigning, and sometimes we had separate efforts, like Jeanne's work for the Women's Center in Carbondale. This working for others became important in the healing process. It is easy to slip into the "I'm-sorry-for-myself" self-absorption, causing endless and purposeless grief. Instead I look back on thirty-nine years with gratitude and a slowly growing understanding of how our shared service to others made our lives so rich.

This is being typed right after the Christmas holidays. Those were tougher days. And an empty house at any time still presents difficulties. But in the midst of writing this a man called with a minor problem concerning his son. He did not know where to turn for help. I don't believe I have met him, but I made a phone call and got his problem worked out. I helped him, but in a strange way he also helped me, taking my focus away from myself to helping others.

That would please Jeanne.

Paul Simon, former U.S. Senator from Illinois, is now director of the Public Policy Institute at Southern Illinois University in Carbondale. He was married to Jeanne from 1960 until her death in 2000.

∝

If my husband, Jimmy, had lived, we would have just celebrated our fifty-fourth wedding anniversary. We were blessed to have 35 of those years with each other. We had a very good marriage, sharing the same values that we instilled in our six children, who in turn took those values into their own marriages and walks of life.

Jimmy was my rock. As the children were growing up, in small crises and times of sickness, I would fall apart. But he would always stay calm and tell me, "Everything will be all right," and I knew it would be.

Then Jimmy himself got sick, and even to that, he tried to shield me. The day he learned he had to go to the hospital for tests, he said to the family, "Don't tell your mother about this until she has her tea and dessert." Later he gently broke the news to me. When the doctors told us Jimmy, my rock, had a brain tumor and only eight months to live, I was devastated. But somehow I found the inner strength to live side by side with him during those last months, never letting him know I knew how sick he really was.

In these years since Jimmy died, I never stop missing him, but I still feel him so much a part of my life. Often I find myself saying to the family, "What would Daddy say about that?" or "Grandpa would be so proud of you." I know it is the love we shared and God's grace that sustain me so that I can still be happy with our children and all 19 of our grandchildren. Ah yes, Jimmy, my rock, is with me still!

—Agnes Gaughan
Bronx, New York

∝

Roses: A Love Story

BY ANONYMOUS

Red roses were her favorites,
her name was also Rose.
And every year her husband sent them,
tied with pretty bows.

The year he died,
the roses were delivered to her door.
The card said, "Be my Valentine,"
like all the years before.

Each year he sent her roses,
and the note would always say,
"I love you even more this year,
than last year on this day.

My love for you will always grow,
with every passing year."
She knew this was the last time
that the roses would appear.

She thought he ordered roses
in advance before this day.
Her loving husband did not know,
that he would pass away.

He always liked to do things early,
way before the time.
Then, if he got too busy,
everything would work out fine.

She trimmed the stems,
and placed them in a very special vase.
Then, sat the vase
beside the portrait of his smiling face.

She would sit for hours,
in her husband's favorite chair.
While staring at his picture,
and the roses sitting there.

A year went by,
and it was hard to live without her mate.
With loneliness and solitude,
that had become her fate.

Then, the very hour,
as on Valentines before,
The doorbell rang, and there were roses,
sitting by her door.

She brought the roses in,
and then just looked at them in shock.
Then, went to get the telephone,
to call the florist shop.

The owner answered, and she asked him,
if he would explain,
Why would someone do this to her,
causing her such pain?

"I know your husband passed away,
more than a year ago,"
The owner said, "I knew you'd call,
and you would want to know.

The flowers you received today,
were paid for in advance.
Your husband always planned ahead,
he left nothing to chance.

There is a standing order,
that I have on file down here,

And he has paid, well in advance,
you'll get them every year.
There also is another thing,
that I think you should know,

He wrote a special little card . . . he did this years ago.
Then, should ever I find out that he's no longer here,
That's the card . . . that should be sent,
to you the following year."

She thanked him and hung up the phone,
her tears now flowing hard.
Her fingers shaking,
as she slowly reached to get the card.

Inside the card, she saw
that he had written her a note.
Then, as she stared in total silence,
this is what he wrote . . .

"Hello my love,
I know it's been a year since I've been gone,
I hope it hasn't been too hard
for you to overcome.

I know it must be lonely,
and the pain is very real.
Or if it was the other way,
I know how I would feel.

The love we shared made everything
so beautiful in life.
I loved you more than words can say,
you were the perfect wife.

You were my friend and lover,
you fulfilled my every need.

I know it's only been a year,
but please try not to grieve.

I want you to be happy,
even when you shed your tears.
That is why the roses will
be sent to you for years.

When you get these roses,
think of all the happiness,
That we had together,
and how both of us were blessed.

I have always loved you
and I know I always will.
But, my love, you must go on,
you have some living still.

Please . . . try to find happiness,
while living out your days.
I know it is not easy,
but I hope you find some ways.

The roses will come every year,
and they will only stop,
When your door's not answered,
when the florist stops to knock.

He will come five times that day,
in case you have gone out.
But after his last visit,
he will know without a doubt,

To take the roses to the place,
where I've instructed him.
And place the roses where we are,
together once again."

They that love beyond the world cannot be separated by it. Death is but crossing the world, as friends do the seas; they live in one another still.

—William Penn

Kindness

I would like to have engraved inside every wedding band, "Be kind to one another." This is the golden rule of marriage, and the secret of making love last through the years.

—Rudolph Ray

Camille offers kindness without my asking for it. There's a line I love. "Living in the country of consideration." She is a considerate human being, and that's really important. I never had that before. I'm glad I've got it now.

—Kelsey Grammer, married to Camille
Donatacci since 1997

I can't tell you what love is. My father explained it to me best when I was growing up. He said, "You have to love everybody." I said, "What do you mean? What about Dougan next door, who drinks and yells at us? I've gotta like Dougan?" He said, "No, no, you don't get it. You don't have to like Dougan. He's a pain in the ass. But you do have to love him. Look, let me put it simply: Just don't do anything to hurt him." When it comes to other people—particularly the other person you share your life and children with—if you try not to hurt them, it's a pretty good start.

—Mel Gibson, married to Robyn since 1980

Be swift to love—make haste to be kind.

—Henri-Frédéric Amiel

Chapter Thirteen

I DO, YOU DO, WE ALL DO—
MARRIAGE IN CULTURE

We are God's work of art.
Ephesians 2:10

The Ten Best Songs about Marriage
You'll Ever Hear
BY JOE DUREPOS

What this really is, is a highly personal, incredibly meaningful selection of
the top ten married songs of all time (or at the very least a pretty good col-

lection of some really sweet songs from mostly the last few years about love and marriage that really turn me on).

I noticed three things when I began to assemble this list. First, agreeing on any top ten list from popular culture—best books, television shows, movies, actors, actresses, athletes, music albums—is a perilous undertaking fraught with the danger of picking from too narrow a band width of time and type. By its very nature, the selection process is highly subjective and ultimately indefensible—except to say, "Hey, that's what I like!" Selecting a list of the top ten married songs is a true challenge. The second thing I noticed is that popular music is filled with songs about *getting* together and shockingly short of songs that celebrate *staying* together.

The editors of *I Like Being® Married* are enthusiastic about celebrating the enduring qualities of a strong marriage. Clearly, the challenge of making a marriage strong and keeping it strong for a long time is not easy. The following songs all attest to that reality. Which leads me to the third thing I noticed in making these selections; that is how few of the songwriters and performers actually found themselves in the kinds of relationships they sing so passionately about—it's a sad footnote.

I want to thank my wife, Betty, for listening to these songs with me— sometimes over and over again to the point of running out of the room holding her ears yelling, "Enough!" She patiently let me argue the merits of each song and was a great sounding board for some of my more questionable picks (if you don't like this list, you should have seen it before she helped me). Part of what gives me a measure of confidence in selecting these songs is the knowledge that I have been married to the same woman I have loved for twenty-two years. Each day, she and I celebrate a little of what's true in each of these songs, and anything I know about the enduring gifts of marriage, I know because she loves me.

The years for the songs reflect their original recording dates. However, the actual recordings listed are the most recent or easiest to find recordings containing the songs should you wish to own a copy for yourself.

1. "When I Said I Do." (Written by Clint Black, 1999, and sung by Clint Black with Lisa Hartman Black, from the *D'lectrified* CD.) This is my favorite song celebrating marriage. Written and sung by Clint Black and accompanied by his wife, Lisa Hartman Black, the song is an honest and

beautiful testament to the enduring commitment at the heart of a great marriage. Wonderful lyrics and a soaring, soulful duet remind us of what we each promised the other in our wedding vows.

2. "Let's Stay Together." (Written by Al Green, Willie Mitchell, and Al Jackson, 1971, as sung by Al Green, from his *Take Me to the River* CD.) A close second to Clint Black's "When I Said I Do," this is a great song, complete with a gospel choir and an infectious beat that makes it hard to sit still while listening to the Reverend Green's heavenly voice imploring his lover to "stay together, loving, whether times are good or bad, happy or sad." A wise prescriptive for what it takes to make a marriage last.

3. "After All." Love theme from *Chances Are,* 1988, by Tom Snow and Dean Pritchford, as sung by Peter Cetera and Cher, from the *You're the Inspiration* CD. My wife Betty's favorite song on this list. It's from the movie *Chances Are*—one of our family's great, guilty video pleasures. "After All" is a ballad about soul mates—the movie's theme is reincarnation—and how each soul falls in love with the same soul every lifetime. I don't know much about reincarnation, but the song speaks to a great romantic notion about the timeless quality of true love.

4. "Do You Love Me?" (Written Jerry Bock and Sheldon Harnick, 1964, from *Fiddler on the Roof.*) From the great Broadway musical, this is the story of the milkman Teyve, his wife, Golde, and their three daughters living a simple life in a small Jewish village in Russia in the time leading up to the revolution. "Do You Love Me?" is sung by Tevye and Golde, after Tevye

has given permission for their middle daughter to marry the young man she loves. It's a witty, wise, and intimate back-and-forth between a long-married couple that transcends time and culture.

5. "Unanswered Prayers." (By Pat Alger, Larry Bastian, and Garth Brooks, 1990, as sung by Garth Brooks, from the *No Fences* CD.) A now happily married man runs into his former girlfriend at a high school football game, triggering memories of nights desperately praying to God that he could marry her, only to find that—fast-forwarding to the present moment—he realizes how lucky he is to be married to his wife and that God's unanswered prayers are sometimes life's greatest blessings.

6. "You're Still the One." (Written by Shania Twain and John "Mutt" Lange, 1997, as sung by Shania Twain, from her *Come On Over* CD.) My wife and I never dated. We fell in love at first sight at a time when age, miles, and circumstances kept us from being together. When we were finally able to get together we quickly married and four years later had our first child. Three children and twenty-two years later it keeps getting better. This song captures the feeling I have for my wife and what we feel when we look back at how far we've come together.

7. "Ribbon in the Sky." (Written and sung by Stevie Wonder, 1982, from *Song Review—A Greatest Hits Collection*.) This is another highly personal choice. It rests on the beautiful wedding day of my wife's sister Kay, where "Ribbon in the Sky" was her choice for her wedding dance song. Hearing it in that moment the song has become for me a celebration of the loving commitment made by two people in a marriage—with the acknowledgment of God as a witness and helper.

8. "Love and Marriage." (Written by Sammy Cahn and James Van Huesen, 1965, as sung—of course!—by Frank Sinatra, from the *Sinatra Reprise: The Very Good Years* CD.) This classic playful tune as sung by Frank Sinatra is like a children's nursery rhyme that pretty much sums up the whole marriage mystery.

9. "Faithfully." (By Jonathan Cain, 1983, as sung by Steve Perry and Journey from their *Greatest Hits* CD). Another personal favorite, this heart-

felt ballad speaks to the difficulties of lovers being away from each other and the joy of rediscovering their love each time they come together again. The most important part of the relationship is that they both remain faithful no matter how much time or how many miles keep them apart. Steve Perry's incredible singing conveys the longing and hope of deeply missing someone you truly love.

10. "Annie's Song." (Written and sung by John Denver, 1975, from *The Best of John Denver Live* CD). I'm forty-five as I write this. For many of my generation who came of age in the seventies, John Denver's beautiful ballad to his lovely wife Annie, remains one of the most romantic professions of love we know. Embodied in the song's lyrics is a depth of feeling, wonder, and awe in loving someone so much you can't imagine living without them.

CHATTERS' CHOICE

America Online asked 143,000 subscribers to name the top ten love songs of all time. Here are their picks:

1. "Amazed," Lonestar
2. "Unchained Melody," Righteous Brothers
3. "I Knew I Loved You," Savage Garden
4. "(Everything I Do) I Do It for You," Bryan Adams
5. "All My Life," K-Ci & JoJo
6. "I Will Always Love You," Whitney Houston or Dolly Parton
7. "This I Promise You," 'N Sync
8. "Truly Madly Deeply," Savage Garden
9. "My Heart Will Go On," Celine Dion
10. "(God Must Have Spent) A Little More Time on You," 'N Sync

—Reported in *USA Today*,
June 1, 2000

Joe Durepos, a literary agent, lives with his wife, Betty, son, Drew, and daughters Clare and Lucy in Downers Grove, Illinois. He and Betty have been married since 1979.

⌒⌾⌒

The Ten Best Books about Marriage You'll Ever Read

BY DANA MACK

1. *Pride and Prejudice* (1813). Jane Austen's most famous novel earns its reputation for being the ultimate "woo and swoon" narrative of courtship. But there is more to this story than just the happy-end romance of Elizabeth Bennet and Mr. Darcy. Austen has created a subtle and searching look at both the right and the wrong reasons for marrying. Indeed, her acrid eye exposes the foibles of old married couples as well as young courting pairs. Elizabeth's parents, for example, are precariously mismatched—her mother an overly self-indulgent woman, her father a somewhat cynical, passive man. Their failure to discipline the younger children of the family very nearly leads to its ruin. Trust it to the heroine's aunt and uncle to provide the model for a match of refined sensibilities and union of purpose.

2. *The Last Chronicle of Barset* (1866). In this masterly novel—the last in Anthony Trollope's Barsetshire series—several very different marital relationships are portrayed. One involves an ambitious woman who demoralizes her husband with henpecking and intrigues; another

involves an indigent clergyman whose pride and eccentricity drive his loving wife near to desperation; yet a third involves a high-rolling couple who come to ruin. There is a model marriage in this tale—a peaceful melding of noble and generous souls. Trollope was a brilliant observer of humanity, and his reflections on matrimony remind us that a marriage is only as solid as the two people in it.

3. *Daniel Deronda* (1876). George Eliot's last work dissects a marriage of convenience turned emotionally abusive. A beautiful girl believes her loveless marriage to a wealthy aristocrat will shore up her family's failing financial resources and bring her the rewards of rank. But Gwendolen Grandcourt, who is used to easily manipulating the gentlemen in her life, has tragically miscalculated her husband's power and potential for cruelty. Brilliant, complex, and poignant, this book traces the story of a relationship doomed by arrogance and idleness.

4. *Anna Karenina* (1877). One of the great novels of all time, Leo Tolstoy's *Anna Karenina* traces the tragic path of an adulterous passion fed at least in part by a woman's feeling of entrapment in an oppressive marriage. This novel, however, also provides a contrasting portrait of a marriage based on perfect sympathy. Tolstoy's subtle character portrayal and his deep ruminations on forgiveness and the moral existence have made this book life-changing for many a reader.

5. *Madame Bovary* (1856). Most people read this famous work by Gustave Flaubert in high school. In a way, that's a shame, since it probably takes more experience of life to properly appreciate. Indeed, it is assigned to students as a critique of nineteenth-century bourgeois society, but it is a lot more than simply a censure of middle-class pretensions. There is much pathos in this story, and a profound understanding of the way unrealistic expectations of marriage can eat away at the emotional life.

6. *Dona Flor and Her Two Husbands* (1969). Brazilian novelist Jorge Amado wrote this exotic and elegant comic fantasy about a remarried widow haunted by the memory of her irresponsible but irresistibly sexy first husband. The work treats some fascinating themes, among them: How important is sex in marriage? Which type of man can inspire greater love,

the proverbial "steady Eddy" (Dona Flor's second husband) or the wild and crazy con man she married first? Dona Flor loves and wants them both.

7. *To the Lighthouse* (1927). This milestone of modernism was written by Virginia Woolf. She uses the "stream of consciousness" technique to slowly unveil the emotional richness of a marriage between two very different people: a brooding, intellectual man, and an active, in-the-world woman. If you are married with children, you'll find this book a particularly penetrating look at both the rewards and challenges of fulfilling our roles as husbands, wives, mothers, and fathers. It's a demanding read, but don't give up. And keep a handkerchief close by; it is bound to move you.

8. *Love and Other Infectious Diseases* (1990). Film critic Molly Haskell's witty and touching memoir, published in 1990, traces her husband's mysterious viral illness, an illness that landed him in the hospital for several months in the early '80s. This frank and clear-sighted account of the emotional strains involved in dealing with both an ailing spouse and a legion of medical professionals is an eloquent contemporary testimony to marital devotion.

9. *Love and Marriage* (1987). Here is Bill Cosby's hilariously funny romantic autobiography, an able reckoning of the typical battle scars we can all expect in the eternal war of the sexes. If you don't find moments to relate to in this wise and true to life compendium of comic incidents, you've never been young or old, never been in love or been married, and have never known anyone who's been in love or married. Reading this book, I had the weird feeling at times that Cosby has been spying on my husband and me. My favorite line: "For two people in a marriage to live together day after day is unquestionably the one miracle the Vatican has overlooked."

10. *The Oxford Book of Marriage* (1990). This wonderful anthology, edited by Helge Rubinstein, is a collection of prose excerpts, poems, epigrams, and letters, all on the subject of marriage, and all selected with an eye to literary excellence. Here are the greatest writers and some of the greatest figures in history on the greatest of subjects: everlasting love! This is a book you can pick up hundreds of times—full of inspiration, insight, and fun.

Dana Mack is editor of *The Book of Marriage: The Wisest Answers to the Toughest Questions* and author of *The Assault on Parenthood: How Our Culture Undermines the Family*. She lives in Wilton, Connecticut.

⸙

Levin had been married three months. He was happy, but not in the way he had expected. At every step he found that he was disappointed in his former dreams and discovered new and unexpected enchantments. Levin was happy, but having embarked on married life, he saw at every step that it was not at all what he had imagined. At every step he experienced what a man experiences when, after admiring the smooth, happy motion of a boat on a lake, he finds himself sitting in it himself. He found that it was not enough to sit quietly without rocking the boat, that he had constantly to consider what to do next, that not for a moment must he forget what course to steer or that there was water under his feet, that he had to row, much as it hurt his unaccustomed hands, that it was pleasant enough to look at it from the shore, but very hard, though very delightful, to sail it.

—Leo Tolstoy, *Anna Karenina*

⸙

The Ten Best Movies about Marriage You'll Ever See

BY MICHAEL LEACH

1. *Tarzan and His Mate* (1934) and *Tarzan Finds a Son* (1939). A first-place tie—these two movies represent the best dream of the nuclear family Hollywood ever made. And they're still a romantic rush to your "jungular" vein. I've seen them both eight million times. As a kid I fantasized about being Boy and living with Tarzan and Jane in a treetop castle where there is always love and protection and fun. As a teenager I focused on the infamous scenes where Maureen O'Sullivan swims naked, and Johnny Weissmuller wakes her in the morning by blowing in her ear while she says, "Oh Tarzan,

you're a bad boy!" As an adult I cherish how nothing stands in the way of Jane and Tarzan's love for each other, their child, and all living things around them. At the fadeout Jane sums it all up: "*Always* is just beginning for you and me." Accept no substi-

tutes; Johnny Weissmuller and Maureen O'Sullivan have it all!

2. *Fargo* (1996). You're darned tootin' this is one of the best! The marriage of Marge Gunderson, a pregnant cop, and her husband Norm stands out like a warm blanket of snow at midnight in this fable about a car salesman who hires thugs to kidnap *his* wife. Marge and Norm (who cooks breakfast and warms up Marge's car each morning) are the still, loving center in the middle of a storm. They share the good of God—peace, assurance, grati- tude, and love—in a mad world. After Marge catches one of the murderous thugs, she makes an observation to him that comes straight from the soul of her marriage: "There's more to life than a little money, ya know. Don'tcha know that? And here you are. And it's a beautiful day. Well, I just don't un- derstand it." In the last scene, before going to sleep, Marge comforts Norm, who came in second place in an art contest. He says, "I love you, Marge." She says, "I love you, Norm." They both say, "Two more months . . ." and fall asleep in peace.

3. *Guess Who's Coming to Dinner* (1967) Ten Academy Award nominations went to this movie that challenged whites and blacks alike to test the sincer- ity of their convictions on integration. Spencer Tracy and Katharine Hepburn play a long-married couple who gets a surprise when their daugh- ter brings home her fiancé for their approval. Well, he may be Sidney Poitier but still he is black and it is 1967. Tracy and the father of the potential groom sound out all the arguments against their children's marriage standing a chance in a segregated society. After a long night's journey into day, Tracy—

and everyone else—sees the light: "In the final analysis it doesn't matter a damn what we think. The only thing that matters is what they feel and how much they feel for each other. And if it's half of what we felt, that's everything." Spencer then gazes at Kate. Those were Tracy's last movie words.

4. *Peggy Sue Got Married* (1986). This pastel of a movie asks: Knowing what you know now about your marriage, would you do things differently if you could begin your life again as a high school senior? Forty-two-year-old Peggy Sue (Kathleen Turner), who is separated from Charlie (Nicolas Cage), gets that chance. Going back in time, she takes new turns but can't help gravitating to Charlie, whose heart is bigger than his flaws. At one point Peggy Sue asks her grandfather if he would do anything differently if he could go back in time. "Well," he answers, "I'd have taken better care of my teeth." In a moving climax Peggy Sue shows the teenage Charlie a locket with photos of their future children. He tells her in bewilderment that they are photos of themselves when they were children! When Peggy Sue comes back to the present, she gives Charlie a second chance. This sweet movie, and its haunting music, will stay with you for years.

5. *Avalon* (1990). Writer/director Barry Levinson's tribute to three generations of an immigrant family is at once a celebration of the extended family and a record of its slow demise due to suburban migration and the spell of television. "What's a first cousin twice removed?" a child asks in the halcyon days when a Thanksgiving meal featured a dozen adults at the big table and just as many children crowded around the small table. In these *Avalon* days of the 1950s we see diverse families supporting each other and caring for each other, but also feeling suffocated and wanting to get away from each other. Yet always, even when they part, we know that they love each other. *Avalon* makes us fondly remember the good old days without feeling nostalgic for them. It is a memory of marriage and family that is real.

6. *Parenthood* (1989). Director Ron Howard and screenwriters Lowell Ganz and Babaloo Mandel (who have fifteen children among them) bring the extended family and the nuclear family together in this tender suburban comedy. Steve Martin plays a loving but harried father who tries to please

everybody, and just can't. His grandmother reveals to him what marriage and family (and the movie) are all about. "You know, when I was nineteen, Grandpa took me on a roller coaster," she remembers. "Up, down, up, down. Oh, what a ride! I always wanted to go again. You know, it was just so interesting to me that a ride could make me so frightened, so scared, so sick, so excited, and so thrilled all together! Some didn't like it. They went on the merry-go-round. That just goes around. Nothing. I like the roller coaster. You get more out of it."

7. *Shadowlands* (1993). Anthony Hopkins is C. S. Lewis, the scholar and author of the *Chronicles of Narnia* and *Mere Christianity*—a bachelor who has spent a lifetime pondering profound truths. Suddenly a deep friendship comes into his life, unexpected and unbidden, in the form of Joy Gresham, an American divorcee. When Joy develops cancer, Lewis proposes to her as she lies sick in a hospital. She improves and they marry in the church and live together as man and wife, in sickness and in health, for four years until Joy's passing in 1960. C. S. Lewis would later write in *A Grief Observed*: "What was [Joy] to me? She was my daughter and my mother, my pupil and my teacher, my subject and my sovereign; and always, holding all these in solution, my trusty comrade, friend, shipmate, fellow-soldier. My mistress; but at the same time all that any man friend (and I have good ones) has ever been to me. Perhaps more. If we had never fallen in love we should have none the less been always together, and created a scandal." If you watch this movie on video, don't just have a handkerchief ready, bring a beach towel.

8. *Father of the Bride* (1950) and *Father of the Bride* (1991). One warm-hearted comedy about a father's letting go of his little girl deserves another, and both of these movies deliver the goods. The difference between them is not only the difference between Spencer Tracy and Steve Martin as the fathers, both of whom are wonderful in their own ways, but between sentiment and sentimentality. In short, the former is Classic Coke, the real thing, and the latter is New Coke, a marketing idea that is nonetheless sweet to the taste. But the new version also has Martin Short as a wild and crazy wedding coordinator, and both movies touch the heart whether you like it or not.

9. *Lovers and Other Strangers* (1970). "So, what's the story?" the patriarch, Frank, played by Richard Castellano, wants to know. The stories are many in this *Nashville* of marriage movies. One of Frank's sons is getting married, the other is considering divorce. The wedding provides a humorous setting for us to learn the stories of the couple's parents, relatives, and friends. The Academy Award–winning song "For All We Know" hints that while we may not know the answer to the father's question, we do understand the love that drives it.

10. *Moonstruck* (1987). "When the moon hits your eye like a big pizza pie, that's amore!" A New York moon works magic on Cher and Nicolas Cage in this romantic comedy about a widow who has given up looking for love, and finds it when she least expects it. Dean Martin love songs tickle our hearts and arias from *La Boheme* send our souls soaring as the unlikely couple discovers their destiny. "The past and the future is a joke to me now," says the passionate Cage. "I see that they're nothing. I see they ain't here. The only thing that's here is you—and me." "La bella luna!" cries Cher's grandfather who has been there, done that, and hasn't forgotten. Neither shall we.

Honorable mentions:

Bill Cosby, Himself (1982). A lovable comic actor simply sits on a chair and shares stories about his marriage and family. A filmed concert performance, it is hilarious as Cos plays the roles of his wife and son and daughters as well as himself. If you appreciated the values in the first *Cosby Show* and enjoyed his books *Love and Marriage* and *Fatherhood*, you will love this movie from whence they sprung. Favorite bit: when his wife wakes up sick and asks him to make breakfast for the kids, Cos literally lets them eat cake. She is not amused. But you will be.

National Lampoon's Vacation (1983). Let's just admit it: The Griswald family's pilgrimage to Wally World is *every* family's vacation. What man cannot identify with Chevy Chase as Clark: well meaning, imperfect, an organizer, a klutz, a loving husband with a careless eye, a caring father who tries too hard, a loser and a hero, a fool and a saint. And what wife would not agree?

When his children ask him why they aren't flying to Wally World, Griswald answers, "Because getting there is half the fun." This movie is nothing but fun.

Only the Lonely (1991). John Candy is a lovable cop who lives with his possessive Irish mother, played by Maureen O'Hara. When he falls in love with a shy woman (Ali Sheedy) who not only works as a mortician's assistant but is Sicilian, John has to make the biggest decision of his life: to stay with Mom or leave home and become one with his wife. After throwing up obstacles, Mom not only comes around but meets her own match in neighbor Anthony Quinn, who teaches her "lust for life" (who else?). The movie features one of the most romantic dates in movie history. Candy treats Sheedy to a picnic in Comiskey Park, just the two of them, late at night, with fireworks that light up the night.

The Sundowners (1960). Robert Mitchum and Deborah Kerr play Australian migrant workers whose home is wherever they are. "Everybody has a hard time of it," Deborah tells her son. But she and her family appreciate life on the spot where they're standing. Not much happens in the movie except little expressions of love and kindness. And that is more than enough.

⚜

Loretta, I love you. Not like they told you love is, and I didn't know this either, but love don't make things nice—it ruins everything. It breaks your heart. It makes things a mess.

We aren't here to make things perfect. The snowflakes are perfect. The stars are perfect. Not us. Not us! We are here to ruin ourselves and to break our hearts and love the wrong people and die.

I love you!

—Nicolas Cage to Cher in *Moonstruck*

Snap out of it!

—Cher as Loretta

∾∞∿

The Ten Best TV Shows about Marriage You'll Ever Watch

BY DAVID BIANCULLI

1. *The Cosby Show* (1984–92, NBC). The TV sitcom was rumored dead until this mammoth hit came along, establishing Father as someone who really *did* know best (and whose wife knew even better). After a decade of comedy in which kids seemed to rule the roost, Bill Cosby's Cliff Huxtable took charge, reacting with loving indignation to his children's poor grades, wacky dates, and loving holiday talent shows.

2. *The Honeymooners* (1955–56, CBS). How can a sitcom in which the husband constantly threatens spousal abuse ("Bang, zoom!") and spends most of each episode deceiving his wife, planning scheme after scheme, be considered as one of the best shows on marriage? Easy. Because this marriage, starring Jackie Gleason and Audrey Meadows as Ralph and Alice Kramden, showed that the institution wasn't easy. Life, for the Kramdens, was a dingy apartment in Brooklyn on his meager salary as a bus driver, and times were tough; the ironic title suggested that the honeymoon was over long ago. Yet at the end of every episode, Ralph saw the error of his ways and told Alice, "Baby, you're the greatest," and deeply meant it.

3. *The Dick Van Dyke Show*. (1961–66, CBS). Even though they had double beds, you know the Petries had an active marriage in more than just the dinner-party sense. Comedy writer Rob (Dick Van Dyke) and house-

wife Laura (Mary Tyler Moore) were like a suburban Jack and Jackie Kennedy: young, attractive, charming, and quintessentially of the '60s. They hugged and kissed often, they were attentive parents, and they had a relationship that clearly was based on love, friendship, and a shared sense of humor.

4. *Mad About You* (1992–99, NBC). Perhaps the best single-series primer on marriage of them all, this sitcom covered all the bases during its seven-year run. It began with Paul and Jamie (Paul Reiser, Helen Hunt) as a recently married couple with separate professional lives, enjoying and exploring everyday married life after the novelty has worn off. Four years into the series, Jamie had an affair and they almost broke up; the next year, they had a baby, Mabel. In the series finale, a grown-up Mabel (Janeane Garofalo), from the fast-forward perspective of the next generation, told a tale in which her parents split up, then ultimately reunited.

5. *The Waltons* (1972–81, CBS). This drama series, set during the Depression, starred Richard Thomas as John-Boy, a man looking back on his family memories (the same structure used, coincidentally, for *Mama*). The parents, played by Ralph Waite as John and Michael Learned as Olivia, didn't dominate many of the story lines (not with seven TV children stealing scenes each week), but their work ethic—he at the sawmill, she at home—was a constant example of marriage as teamwork.

6. *Mama* (1949–57, CBS). Set at the turn of the century (the twentieth century, that is), this popular Golden Age sitcom starred Peggy Wood as the matriarch of a hard-working Norwegian family living in San Francisco. Whether the problem was balancing the family budget or helping her younger daughter prepare for a spelling bee, this early situation comedy was more interested in presenting and solving the conflicts of family life than reaching for easy laughs.

7. *7th Heaven* (1996–, WB). Defiantly presenting both a nuclear family unit and a religious one at a time when both were virtually nonexistent in TV dramas, this series presents Stephen Collins as a minister with a wife (Catherine Hicks) and seven children. The stories are moral but not overtly

preachy, and the characters, even the minister, are presented with flaws and foibles intact. It's a TV marriage where the love between the spouses, and the love for the children, is never in question.

8. *The Adventures of Ozzie and Harriet* (1952–66, ABC). This show makes the cut because, unlike all other series on this list, it was a marriage on TV in the most literal sense: Ozzie Nelson and his apron-wearing housewife Harriet were married in real life, portraying themselves. They starred in this genial sitcom, portraying a world in which the parents, between and sometimes during family meals, worked together to solve the problems and squabbles of their kids—played by their real sons, David and Ricky.

9. *The Bob Newhart Show* (1972–78, CBS). Most shows on this list are about people who are married with children. Bob Newhart never went that route on this hit CBS sitcom, in which he played psychologist Bob Hartley. He and wife, Emily, played by Suzanne Pleshette, were the only two members of their household (at least once the neighbors left). Emily, like Bob, had a daytime job (she was an elementary school teacher), but the two always found time to do things together, discuss the day, and wind up lying next to each other in bed.

10. *He & She* (1967–68, CBS). Like the Nelsons on *The Adventures of Ozzie and Harriet*, this series starred a husband and wife who were playing a husband and wife—only in this case, Richard Benjamin and Paula Prentiss weren't playing themselves. Their characters, though named Dick and Paula, were the Hollisters. He was a cartoonist, she was a social worker, and he and she had a sexy, vibrant, mutually respectful marriage that was fun to watch.

Honorable mentions:

I Love Lucy (1951–57, CBS), with its real-life married stars and a weekly message that honesty really is the best policy.

Leave It to Beaver (1957–63, CBS and ABC), in which parents Ward and June worked together, behind closed doors, to come up with the best advice to give their trouble-prone boy.

Family (1976–80, ABC), a prime-time family soap covering a husband and wife's triumphs and travails with their offspring and lots of topical issues, from drugs to abortion.

Hart to Hart (1979–84, ABC), a *Thin Man*–type lighthearted mystery series in which the husband-and-wife detective team is rich, glamorous, flirtatious, and deeply in love.

The Simpsons (1990–, Fox), a cartoon in which the seemingly dysfunctional family has at its core a husband and wife who love and need one another, as in *The Honeymooners*.

Everybody Loves Raymond (1996–, CBS), which at bottom is a cautionary tale about living too close to one's parents or in-laws.

Once and Again (1999–, ABC), a very unusual TV show about marriage because the central characters aren't married at all, but are separated or divorced from previous spouses. The valuable message here? Even when a marriage ends, its legacies and complications do not.

David Bianculli is the TV critic for the *New York Daily News* and National Public Radio, and the author of *Teleliteracy: Taking Television Seriously* and *Dictionary of Teleliteracy: Television's 500 Biggest Hits, Misses, and Events*.

Ralph Kramden: I have—I've got an explanation. A perfect one. I'm a dope. Not a run-of-the-mill dope, the world's champ. For years I've been taking for granted the most wonderful thing that's ever happened to me—you. I've never shown you the appreciation you deserve, Alice. You could walk outta that door right now and I wouldn't blame you. You deserve something better than me. There are a million guys who'd give you anything if they could have a girl like you.

Alice: Ralph, I don't want a million. There's just one guy I want: you.

Ralph: Baby, you're the greatest!

—*The Honeymooners*

From This Day Forward

BY COKIE AND STEVE ROBERTS

We're big fans of marriage and don't apologize for that. We have always agreed with the author Judith Viorst, who once wrote a book called *Married Is Better*. Not better for everyone, to be sure, but for most people. And we believe strongly that a devoted marriage can be reconciled with individual growth and development. Marriage has enlarged our lives, not encircled them; it has opened new doors, not closed them. We are better people together than we are separately.

But let's be honest. Marriage is serious business and hard work. It's not just becoming roommates, it's becoming soul mates; it's not just signing a license, it's sharing a life. The words in the marriage ceremony "from this day forward" are scary. At the moment a couple exchanges those vows they can never know what they really mean, what hills and valleys stretch out in front of them in the years ahead. But if you take the words seriously, there's no going back. There's only the future, unlimited and unknowable, and the promise to make the journey together.

Chapter Fourteen

SOMETHING OLD, SOMETHING NEW

How rare and wonderful is that flash of a moment when we realize that we have made a difference in the life of another.
—Anthony P. Witham

A Married Couple Looks Back with Love
BY MICHAEL AND VICKIE LEACH

Michael: It was 1968, the year Kennedy and King were killed, the year of burning cities and the Chicago convention. Anything was possible. Even love.

Vickie: I had just moved to New York from Mississippi. I was just out of college, and excited about my first job and life in the big city. On October 25 my roommate Holly and I moved into a tiny apartment in Greenwich Village, our first home away from home. That night Holly suggested we go down the block to a sing-along place called Your Father's Mustache. I was tired but decided to tag along.

Michael: I was twenty-eight, and a Catholic priest. Ever since I was a kid, I had always wanted to be a priest. I wanted to help other people and make them happy, especially children. As a seminarian I dreamt of burning myself out for Christ before I was forty, just like Don Bosco, my favorite saint. When I started to do that, I had second thoughts. I had gotten back to the rectory late at night when my friend Artie called from New York. He was on vacation, and asked me to hop a plane and join him.

"I can't," I said, "I've got work to do."

"When's the last time you had a vacation?" he asked. "Come on. You can see some plays. You love plays. It'll be fun."

He talked me into it. When I got to the hotel, the desk man gave me a note. It said, "Meet me at Your Father's Mustache. In the Village. Seven o'clock."

Vickie: At the time, believe it or not, two guys wanted to marry me. All my life all I ever wanted to be was married, have children, and live in a house with a white picket fence. But I couldn't decide between them. One was my high school sweetheart: he was kind and gentle. The other was my boyfriend from college: he was strong and confident. I remember once asking my mother: "How will I know when I'm really in love?" She said, "You'll know, and you won't have to ask."

Michael: I got to Your Father's Mustache at seven. Artie wasn't there. I stood on the sawdust floor near the back and waited. A band in the front played banjos and a tuba and piano, and everybody in the room drank beer and sang songs like "Those were the days, my friend, we thought they'd never end." I looked at my watch. It was 7:30. Where was Artie?

I just stood there and watched everyone having fun. I noticed two girls sitting at a table against the wall. One was blond, the other brunette. They were both pretty but the brunette was stunning. She had long dark hair and wore a poncho like Clint Eastwood in *Fistful of*

Dollars. She was singing and swaying with such joy. I couldn't take my eyes off her.

Vickie: My roommate Holly was blond and gorgeous, she could have been a model. I said to her, "There's a guy near the bar, and he's looking at you."

Michael: And then I did something I had never done before. Here I was, a priest who had always kept the rules, and what did I do? I went and asked the bartender for a pitcher of beer. Then I walked over to the table and asked the girls, "Would you like some beer?" I couldn't believe I was doing this. It was all in slow motion.

Vickie: I couldn't believe it. He sat in front of *me.*

Michael: She was magic. I noticed that her eyes were different colors. One was hazel and specked with green, and the other a cloudy blue.

Vickie: When I was a baby I fell on a glass toy. It broke and cut my eye. I was blind in that eye and looked like a freak. When we played games, I was always the bad guy or the monster. As I got older, adults looked at me and recoiled. I used to beg God for a miracle so I could look like everybody else. Sure, I had two boyfriends but I didn't know how anyone could *really* love me the way I was.

Michael: She was beautiful. Still is.

Vickie: He was handsome. I asked him what he did.

Michael: I told her, "I'm a priest."

Vickie: I roared! I had never heard that before! The best thing was, I knew he was telling the truth.

Michael: I loved it that she laughed. Artie came in and sat next to Holly and they sang while Vickie and I tried to talk over the music. After half an hour I asked her if she'd like to take a walk.

Vickie: We walked around the Village for hours. I told him about my eye and about my boyfriend dilemma and how I didn't know what to do. I had grown up Catholic and went to Catholic schools but Michael was totally different from any priest I'd ever met. I didn't see him as a priest. He was just the kindest person I'd ever known.

Michael: It was one of those beautiful October nights when the air is crisp and clean and you can see things a mile away. Vickie told me that one of the guys who wanted to marry her was strong and that the other one was gentle, and that she couldn't make up her mind between the two.

She was so good. I said she deserved to find someone who had both qualities.

Vickie: And I thought: "I'm looking at him."

Michael: I told her how I loved working with kids but how it was also lonely and that I'd been thinking about what it would be like to marry someone and have children of our own. We walked and talked until about two in the morning. I walked her home.

Vickie: We climbed the stairs, sat on a step, and talked some more. I was thinking of what my mother told me: "You'll know and you won't have to ask."

Michael: Then I asked her something I hadn't asked since Sally Brightman in ninth grade. I asked her, "May I kiss you?"

Vickie: It was the perfect ending of a perfect night.

Michael: The next day I took a subway to her office and asked the lady up front to give her a package. Vickie had told me how she grew up living over her father's bakery in a small town, so I wrapped up a chocolate-covered doughnut with a red rose in a gift box.

Vickie: Every day at noon for three days he came with a different present; we had lunch on a park bench or in a diner that was as romantic to us as the Taj Mahal. And every night we went out. One night he took me to *Man of La Mancha,* and I thought that he was Don Quixote and I was Dulcinea and that we were living an impossible dream.

Michael: I remember after the show, walking down Broadway, holding her hand, and thinking, "I am walking through a neon-colored dream with this beautiful, wonderful girl. I can't believe this is happening, but I could do it for the rest of my life." Remember that orange chiffon miniskirt you wore?

Vickie: It was pink.

Michael: I remember orange.

Vickie: You always do.

Michael: On the fourth day she had a touch of the flu and couldn't go to work. I got her a tuna fish sandwich, her favorite food, and went to her apartment. I sat by her bedside and told her a story.

Vickie: "The Tattooed Boy."

Michael: It was a story I had first told years ago to kids at Angel Guardian Orphanage. I loved to tell them stories. I'd just start and a story would come out. This one was about Christopher Holiday, a boy with bat's ears and bat's tears and a little clown's frown. Envious people had tattooed him because they were afraid of the love and goodness in him. Christopher wore a clown's suit and worked at a freak show. One night he decided to run away. But before he left the carnival grounds, he came across another little boy, sitting on the edge of the carousel, who also wore a clown's suit and looked just like him—with bat's ears and bat's tears and a little clown's frown! He asked the boy, in astonishment, who he was. The boy was confident and loving and said to him, "Look into my eyes! Look into my eyes and you'll see who I really am!"

Christopher looked into his eyes. And what he saw was a perfect image of himself. He began to love himself the way the boy on the carousel first loved him.

That's how Christ loves us, I told the kids, and that's how it was with Vickie and me.

Vickie: I didn't want him to go back to Chicago.

Michael: I told her, "I've got All Saints' Day on Sunday. I have to go back. We have to be mature. This is crazy. We mustn't call each other for a month."

Vickie: He called me the night he got back. A year later, in October, we got married in a church in Greenwich Village.

Soon after we married I got an infection in my eye. The bad eye was

"You could see things a mile away..."

causing problems and had to be removed. The eye was removed and I received an artificial one that made me look just like everyone else. It was another gift from God. All my dreams, all my prayers, had come true.

Michael: You don't have a white picket fence.

Vickie: We have each other and two wonderful sons, and we're one. We don't need a fence.

Michael: Life hasn't always been easy, but we've had no more than three or four quarrels in 32 years. And none lasted more than a few hours. I can't remember when the last one was.

Vickie: There's nothing worth arguing about.

Michael: We've grown into that wonderful stage where we think each other's thoughts and feel each other's feelings and say the same things at the same time. There's

"Look into my eyes and you'll see who I really am..."

always an uneasy thought lurking in the back of our mind that someday one of us will get sick and die, but we believe that what is good and beautiful in us will always live and always be together as one.

Vickie: I just live moment by moment and am grateful to God every day.

Michael: And I still can't believe how lucky I am. First you fall in love. That's the exciting part. Then you learn to love. That's the hard part. Finally, you simply love being loving. That, by far, is the best part.

Vickie: You taught me how to love others.

Michael: You taught me how to love myself.

Vickie: It's all the same.

Michael: Are you sure that dress wasn't orange?

Vickie: It was pink.

Michael: It was beautiful.

Vickie: Yes. It still is.

c∞ɔ

A Married Couple Looks Forward with Hope

BY THERESE AND ERIC BORCHARD

Therese: It was autumn, 1994, and I was horribly depressed. Only three weeks after I had left home and moved to Chicago for my first big job, I knew it was a bad fit. My boss hated me. My colleagues made fun of me. And I learned my dad was dying three hundred miles away. What was I doing here?

Eric: Life was pretty good for me. After two years in the Windy City, I had made some friends, landed a job as an architect for a new firm, and found an affordable one-bedroom apartment in Oak Park with a skyline view.

Therese: I commuted home to Dayton, Ohio, most weekends to see my dad. But the weekend of October first I stuck around to visit with Libby, a college friend who had come up from South Bend, Indiana. She wanted to introduce me to a friend of hers who had "the same sense of humor" as I do. I appreciated her good intentions, but my funny bone was broken, and my self-esteem was dwindling as fast as a helium balloon floating in the air three weeks after the party.

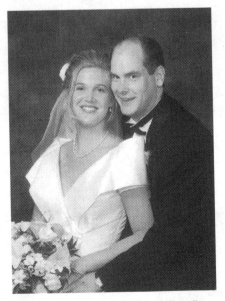

Eric: I was enjoying a quiet Saturday when Libby called and invited me over to meet her friend in Lincoln Park. My first thought was parking—or the lack of it in that neighborhood. So I almost said no. But when she put Therese on the phone to give me directions, I was intrigued. She sounded nervous.

"I tried to be the best friend I could be..."

Therese: I was.

208

Eric: I showed up with a cheap bottle of wine. Therese didn't own an opener. Later I learned she hadn't had a drink in over five years. I should have brought flowers.

Therese: Eric didn't score any points with the Mogen David, but he quickly made up for it when, after shaking my hand, he suddenly looked down at his pants and, realizing his fly was down, said with a goofy, impish expression, "Sorry." From then on, we fed off each other like a perfect comedy team. I hadn't laughed so hard since—

Eric: Ever. You told me you had never laughed so hard in your life.

Therese: We had so much chemistry and energy together. When I began a sentence—

Eric: I often ended it. It was spontaneous but I felt like I said all the right things around her. Still do. Therese was the first person who appreciated me for who I was—insecurities and all.

Therese: Same with me. I had just ended the last of my unhealthy relationships, where I tried so hard to be someone else. "Surely, he'll like me if I do this, or look like that," and so on. I was sick of the games. Eric loved me for who I was, and helped me to love myself and see the real beauty inside of me.

Eric: Before meeting Therese, I put a lot of my self worth into my job. My self-esteem would go up and down with each accomplishment or criticism. She made all that is really good in me come alive. Career opportunities come and go, but being in love is something that will even outlast us.

Therese: Shortly after we started dating, my father died. My dad would have loved Eric, and been so proud of my decision. I'm sorry that they never got to meet each other.

Eric: When Therese's dad died, our relationship entered a new stage. We were both confronted with the reality of life and death, which kills all ego games and pretending. Without a support system in a new city, I knew that Therese needed a friend more than anything. I tried to be the best friend I could be.

Therese: I don't know what I would have done without Eric's love and support during that time. My insides were raw, my emotions unfinished. Most men would have surely seen the mess as their exit cue, but Eric stuck around to help me heal. He taught me what real love is. And I knew if we made it past this so early in our relationship, we would make it through anything.

Eric: Therese and I became closer than ever and soon were ready to commit to each other forever. I asked her to marry me on the campus of Saint Mary's College in South Bend, Indiana, her alma mater, on the one-year anniversary of our meeting.

Therese: Ironically, October 1 is the feast day of St. Therese, after whom my mom named me and to whom I've always had a special devotion. I felt as though all of heaven was blessing our life together.

Eric: I just knew it was the right thing to do. I've never felt so sure of anything in my life.

Therese: The theme for our wedding was "love is stronger than death," based on a verse from the Song of Songs in the Bible. It seemed perfect, as both of us were learning about the fragility of life and the endurance of love. My mom walked me "around" the altar—Our Lady of Loretto Church had a modern layout—on the afternoon of June 22, 1996. It was the happiest day of my life.

Eric: I didn't think it could get much better than that. But it has.

Therese: Our marriage is a mutual support system. It makes life easier, even though you have to work at compromising along the way. Eric is

my best friend. I can't think of anyone else I'd rather spend my life with.

Eric: If I were stuck on an abandoned island and could pick one person to be there with me, it would be Therese.

Therese: I didn't think we could get much closer than we were after my dad died, but that was only the beginning. When our first baby was born a few weeks ago, our lives became sewn together by a new life.

Eric: I couldn't talk when I first brought our son to meet his mother after her cesarean. I have never felt so much love in all my life. It was a difficult birth but

"There is nothing more awesome than the miracle of love..."

miraculously this beautiful little person now embodies my love for Therese and her love for me.

Therese: When I look at our son, I love Eric even more. Every day David moves my heart to see the incredible miracle of love waiting to be born inside each of us.

It is only with the heart
that one can see rightly;
what is essential
is invisible to the eye.

Antoine de St. Exupéry

ACKNOWLEDGMENTS

We are grateful to the many contributors whose original stories illumine this book, and to the publishers who gave us permission to reprint sparkling excerpts from their books, magazines, and newspapers.

We are particularly grateful to Anne Kertz Kernion for her lovely artwork, and for her cheerleading from day one. Anne designs beautiful gift cards. Check them out on www.cardsbyanne.com.

Our special thanks go to Doris Goodnough, Karin Volpe, Donna Caldarola, Janira Quinones, Bishop Robert Morneau, Nancy Lucas, Tom McGrath, and David Morris. For those we failed to mention, we apologize.

We send a great big thank-you to our agent, Joe Durepos, and to all the wonderful professionals at Doubleday: Elizabeth Walter, Trace Murphy, Andrew Corbin, Siobhan Dunn, Liz DeRidder, Lorraine Hyland, Carol Christiansen, Lisa McCormick, Mary Ann Reilly, Alexandra Morris, Rachel Pace, Bette Alexander, Steve Rubin, the entire marketing and sales team, and Eric Major, our publisher.

Most of all, we give great big hugs to Vickie Leach and Eric Borchard. We're grateful that you married us.

Michael Leach is the executive director of Orbis Books. A past president and publisher of the Crossroad/Continuum Publishing Group, he has edited and published close to two thousand books. His authors include Nobel Prize winners, National Book Award winners, and scores of religious book award winners. He has also written and edited a number of books of his own, including *I Like Being® American* and *I Like Being® Catholic,* with Therese J. Borchard. Mike and his wife, Vickie, have two grown children and live in Connecticut.

Therese J. Borchard is the editor of *I Love Being a Mom* and the coeditor, with Michael Leach, of the bestseller *I Like Being® Catholic.* She is a nationally syndicated columnist and has published articles in the *Washington Post, Newsday,* the *Baltimore Sun, American Baby,* and other newspapers and periodicals. Therese holds an M.A. degree in theology from the University of Notre Dame and lives with her husband, Eric, and two children in Annapolis, Maryland.

CREDITS

The editors have endeavored to credit all known persons holding copyright or reproduction rights for passages quoted and for illustrations reproduced in this book, especially:

Boteach. This article first appeared on www.beliefnet.com, the leading multifaith Web site on religion, spirituality, and morality.

Bettmann/CORBIS for photographs of Anne Bancroft and Mel Brooks, and Paul Newman and Joanne Woodward.

Carol Publishing Group, for excerpt from *From Mother to Daughter* by Joan Rivers. Copyright © 1998 by Joan Rivers.

Classic Photos for photographs of the Tarzan family and *The Honeymooners.*

Commonweal magazine, June 18, 1993, Vol. 120, No. 12, for excerpt from "Take Your Shoes Off My Books" by Jo McGowan. Copyright © 1993 by Commonweal Foundation, reprinted with permission. For subscriptions, call toll free: 1–888–495–6755.

Conari Press, for excerpt from *Meant to Be* by Joyce and Barry Vissell, copyright © 2000 by Joyce and Barry Vissell, by permission of Conari Press.

Conari Press, for excerpt from *Weddings from the Heart* by Daphne Rose Kingma, copyright © 1995 by Daphne Rose Kingma, by permission of Conari Press.

The Coretta Scott King Collection, for wedding picture of Dr. Martin Luther King and Coretta King. License granted by Intellectual Properties Management, Atlanta, Georgia, as exclusive licensor of the King estate.

The C. S. Lewis Company Limited, for excerpts from *A Grief Observed* by C. S. Lewis, copyright © C. S. Lewis Pte. Ltd. 1961. Extract reprinted by permission.

David Allocca/DMI/TimePix for photographs of Anne Meara and Jerry Stiller.

The Detroit News, November 3, 1995, for excerpts from Mel Brooks and Anne Bancroft.

Doubleday, a division of Random House, Inc., for excerpts from *Love and Marriage* by Bill Cosby, copyright © 1989 by Bill Cosby. Used by permission of Doubleday, a division of Random House, Inc.

Doubleday, a division of Random House, Inc., for excerpt from *Memoirs* by Mikhail Gorbachev, copyright © 1995 by Mikhail Gorbachev, English translation © by Wolf Jobst Siedler Verlag GmbH, Berlin. Used by permission of Doubleday, a division of Random House, Inc.

Doubleday, a division of Random House Inc., for excerpt from *Please Don't Eat the Daisies* by Jean Kerr, copyright © 1957 by Jean Kerr. Used by permission of Doubleday, a division of Random House, Inc.

Doubleday, a division of Random House, Inc., for excerpt from *Sonnets from the Portuguese and Other Love Poems* by Elizabeth Barrett Browning. Copyright © 1954 by Doubleday and Company, Inc.

Doubleday, a division of Random House, Inc., for excerpt from *You Only Get Married for the First Time Once* by Judy Markey. Copyright © 1988 by Judy Markey.

Good Housekeeping magazine, March 2000, for excerpt from Phil McGraw.

G. P. Putnam's Sons, a division of Penguin Putnam, for excerpt from *It's Not About the Bike* by Lance Armstrong. Copyright © 2000 by Lance Armstrong.

Guideposts magazine, May 1989, August 1990, October 1994, and December 1998, for excerpts from Sue Monk Kidd, Carol Kuykendall, Debbi Smoot, and Linda Ching Sledge.

HarperCollins Publishers, Inc., for 307 word excerpt from *Celine Dion: My Story* by Celine Dion. Copyright © 2000 by Georges-Herbert Germain, Celine Dion, René Angélil, Les Editions Robert Laffont. Reprinted by permission of HarperCollins, Inc.

HarperCollins Publishers, Inc., for excerpt from *Whole Child/Whole Parent, 4th Edition* by Polly Berrien Berends. Copyright © 1975, 1983, 1987, 1997 by Polly Berrien Berends. Foreword copyright © by M. Scott Peck. Reprinted by permission of HarperCollins, Inc.

Harvard University Press, for excerpt from *The Book of Abigail and John: Selected Letters of the Adams Family*. Reprinted by permission of the publisher from *The Adams Papers: Adams Family Correspondence, Volume II*, June 1776 to March 1778, edited by L. H. Butterfield, Cambridge, Mass.: The Belknap Press of Harvard University Press, copyright © 1963 by the Massachusetts Historical Society.

© 1993 Gruner + Jahr USA Publishing. Reprinted from *Parents* magazine by permission.

Random House, Inc., for excerpt from *All's Fair* by Mary Matalin and James Carville. Copyright © 1994 by Mary Matalin and James Carville.

Random House, Inc., for excerpts from *Illuminata* by Marianne Williamson, copyright © 1994 by Marianne Williamson. Used by permission of Random House, Inc.

Random House, Inc., for excerpts from *I Love You, Ronnie* by Nancy Reagan, copyright © 2000 Ronald Reagan Presidential Foundation. Used by permission of Random House, Inc.

Random House, Inc., for excerpt from *My American Journey* by Colin Powell with Joseph E. Persico, copyright © 1995 by Colin Powell. Used by permission of Random House, Inc.

Redbook magazine, for selected quotes from celebrities published in Clint Black/"How We Keep Passion in Our Marriage," April 1999, and November 1999.

RCA, for CD cover of Clint Black/*D'lectrified*: Courtesy of RCA Label Group Nashville. Under license from BMG Special Products.

Robert H. Ferrell, for excerpts from *Off the Record: The Private Papers of Harry S. Truman,* edited by Robert H. Ferrell. Copyright © 1980 by Robert Ferrell. Reprinted with permission of Ann Elmo Agency, Inc.

Roy Rogers, Jr., for photograph of the Roy Rogers family.

Scribner, a division of Simon & Schuster, Inc., for excerpts from *All the Best* by George Bush. Copyright © 1999 by George H. W. Bush. Reprinted with the permission of Scribner, a division of Simon & Schuster, Inc.

Simon & Schuster, for excerpts from *Happy Trails* by Roy Rogers and Dale Evans with Jane and Michael Stern. Copyright © 1994 by Roy Rogers, Dale Evans, Jane Stern, and Michael Stern. Reprinted with the permission of Simon & Schuster.

Simon & Schuster, for excerpt from *Married to Laughter* by Jerry Stiller.

Copyright © 2000 by Jerry Stiller. Reprinted with the permission of Simon & Schuster.

Simon & Schuster, for excerpts from *Napoleon and Josephine: The Biography of a Marriage* by Frances Mossiker. Copyright © 1964 by Frances Mossiker. Reprinted with the permission of Simon & Schuster.

Sky magazine, for excerpt from Mel Gibson. *Sky* magazine, Pace Communications Inc., Greensboro, North Carolina.

Terry Smith/TimePix, for photograph of Shakira Caine.

Thomas D. McAvoy/TimePix, for photograph of Grace Kelly.

Turtle Bay Books, a division of Random House, Inc., for excerpt from *What's It All About?* by Michael Caine, copyright © 1992 by Stoke Films Ltd. Used by permission of Turtle Bay Books, a division of Random House, Inc.

U.S. Catholic, May 1998, for excerpts from "Keeping Love's Promise" by Pattiann Rogers and "As Time Goes By" by Tom McGrath.

Villard Books, a division of Random House, Inc., for excerpt from *Never Die Easy: The Autobiography of Walter Payton* by Walter Payton with Don Yaeger. Copyright © 2000 by Celebrity Appearances, Inc., and Don Yaeger.

Warner Books, Inc., for excerpts from *My Sergei: A Love Story* by Ekaterina Gordeeva. Copyright © 1996 by Ekaterina Gordeeva.

William Morrow, for three excerpts totaling 343 words from *From This Day Forward* by Cokie and Steve Roberts. Copyright © 2000 by Cokie and Steve Roberts. Reprinted by permission of HarperCollins Publishers, Inc., William Morrow.

William Morrow, for selections totaling 1204 words from *With Ossie and Ruby: In This Life Together* by Ossie Davis and Ruby Dee. Copyright © 1998 by Ossie Davis and Ruby Dee. Reprinted by permission of HarperCollins Publishers, Inc., William Morrow.

Printed in the United States
by Baker & Taylor Publisher Services